John Patrick Donnelly

Marquette University

Ignatius of Loyola

Founder of the Jesuits

The Library of World Biography

Series Editor: Peter N. Stearns

PEARSON

Longman

New York   San Francisco   Boston
London   Toronto   Sydney   Tokyo   Singapore   Madrid
Mexico City   Munich   Paris   Cape Town   Hong Kong   Montreal

*This book is dedicated to my
students, past and present.*

Vice President and Publisher: Priscilla McGeehon
Acquisitions Editor: Erika Gutierrez
Executive Marketing Manager: Sue Westmoreland
Production Coordinator: Shafiena Ghani
Project Coordination, Text Design, Electronic Page Makeup, and Art
    Studio: Sunflower Publishing Services
Senior Cover Design Manager/Designer: Nancy Danahy
Cover Image: *Portrait of St. Ignatius* done posthumously by Jacopino
    Del Conte in 1556. Courtesy of the Institute of Jesuit Sources.
Manufacturing Manager: Dennis J. Para
Printer and Binder: RR Donnelley and Sons Company/Harrisonburg
Cover Printer: Coral Graphics, Inc.

Library of Congress Cataloging-in-Publication Data

Donnelly, John Patrick, 1934–
    Ignatius of Loyola: founder of the Jesuits / John Patrick Donnelly.
        p. cm.—(The library of world biography)
    Includes bibliographical references (p.) and index.
    ISBN 0-321-08618-X (pbk.)
    1. Ignatius, of Loyola, Saint, 1491–1556.   2. Christian saints—
Spain—Biography.   I. Title.   II. Series.

BX4700.L7D63 2004
271'.5302—dc21
[B]   2003047567

Please visit our website at http://www.ablongman.com

ISBN 0-321-08618-X

12345678910—DOH—05040302

Contents

Ignatius writes the Jesuit Constitutions.

Editor's Preface

"Biography is history seen through the prism of a person."
—Louis Fischer

It is often challenging to identify the roles and experiences of individuals in world history. Larger forces predominate. Yet biography provides important access to world history. It shows how individuals helped shape the society around them. Biography also offers concrete illustrations of larger patterns, in political and intellectual life, in family life, and in the economy.

The Longman Library of World Biography series seeks to capture the individuality and drama that mark human character. It deals with individuals operating in one of the main periods of world history, while also reflecting issues in the particular society around them. Here, the individual illustrates larger themes of time and place. The interplay between the personal and the general is always the key to using biography in history, and world history is no exception. Always, too, there is the question of personal agency: how much do individuals, even great ones, shape their own lives and environment, and how much are they shaped by the world around them?

Peter Stearns

Author's Preface

Loyola and the Reformation Era

The Reformation was the last period of Western history in which religion and religious questions occupied center stage. Historians usually see the new era beginning when Martin Luther posted his ninety-five theses on the practice and doctrine of indulgences at Wittenberg on 31 October 1517. Much to Luther's surprise, his action stirred enormous interest and quickly led to calling into question far more important teachings and practices of the medieval church than indulgences, first in Germany and gradually through most of Europe. Eventually much of Germany, Switzerland, and the Netherlands and all of Scandinavia, England, and Scotland broke with the Roman Catholic church. Scattered Protestant communities emerged in most other countries west of Russia and north of the Ottoman Empire. History textbooks rightly tend to give more space and stress to what is new in any era. Colorful personalities such as Luther, Ulrich Zwingli, and John Calvin introduced important changes into both religious doctrine and practice; these changes continue to influence religion in the United States and around the world today. Rightly, then, do textbooks on Western civilization give more space to the Protestant Reformation than to religious change that was taking place contemporaneously in Catholic countries.

Still, a case can be made that developments within Roman Catholicism were no less important, even if they were not as radical. The Treaty of Westphalia in 1648 is usually seen as the terminal date of the Reformation era because it ended the Thirty Years War, which was the last, longest, and bloodiest of the Wars of Religion. In 1648 there were more than twice as many Catholics as Protestants in Europe, and in the world today the Catholic numerical advantage has increased. The changes and the momentum for reform in the Roman Catholic church during the life of Ignatius of Loyola largely shaped Catholicism until the Second Vatican Council and the late twentieth century.

Ralph Waldo Emerson claimed, "There is properly no history, only biography." Emerson exaggerates, but to make a valid point. Real history must be about real people, and as Barbara Tuchman has argued, biographies serve as a prism of history and hold our attention because we are interested in other people. But if we are to learn history through a biography, the life of the person studied must encompass and illuminate major themes of his or her times. No one figure in the refashioning of Catholicism during the sixteenth century stands as tall as Ignatius of Loyola. The first published biography of Loyola, written by his friend and disciple Pedro de Ribadeneira (1526–1611), contrasted the roles of Luther (1483–1548) and Loyola (1491–1556) in the Protestant and Catholic Reformations, respectively. They lived almost exactly the same length of time, and their lives largely overlapped. The same Luther-Loyola juxtaposition was even more prominent in the baroque biography of Loyola by another Jesuit, Daniello Bartoli. Published in 1650, it remained popular for three centuries. Peter Paul Rubens, a friend of the Jesuits and the most prolific of baroque artists, did a series of paintings glorifying Loyola in the Jesuit church at Antwerp. Other baroque artists also evoked the heroic image of Loyola, notably in the two main Jesuit churches at Rome, the Gesù and San Ignazio; hundreds of other Jesuit churches contained artworks—paintings, statues, windows—glorifying Loyola and his work, especially after he was declared a saint in 1622. It is little wonder, then, that many historians in their quest for an individual to use as the champion of the Catholic Reformation have fastened on Ignatius of Loyola.

The Catholic response to Protestantism in the period 1540–1650 has often been split into two complimentary drives: the Counter-Reformation (Catholic efforts to combat Protestantism) and the Catholic Reformation (efforts to reform the morals and intensify the piety of both clergy and laypeople). The establishment of the Roman Inquisition and the Index of Forbidden Books, the condemnation of Protestant teaching by the Council of Trent, Catholic polemical writings, and especially the Wars of Religion are usually assigned to the Counter-Reformation. The Catholic Reformation included reform measures voted at Trent, more effective teaching of catechism, the founding of some thirty new religious orders for both men and women, revitalization of older religious orders, better training of clergy in seminaries, efforts to evangelize rural areas, and missionary work in Asia, Africa, and the Americas. Bishops began preaching to their people, and popes put religious reform ahead of politics and art patronage. Loyola was only indirectly concerned with Counter-Reformation efforts to combat Protestantism, although he supported them. He was deeply involved in almost all aspects of reforming Catholicism. No life better illustrates the Catholic Reformation than does Loyola's.

Loyola made two contributions that profoundly influenced his age and continue at work even in our day. He wrote *The Spiritual Exercises,* a book which for centuries has guided people in reforming their lives spiritually. More important, he founded the Society of Jesus, known as the Jesuits, which grew into the most influential religious order of the early modern period and remains the largest Catholic religious order for men.

Textbooks routinely speak of Loyola as the soldier saint. This biography hopes to show that the stereotype of soldier saint is both misleading and lacking historical foundation. Loyola's life (1491–1556) breaks into three distinct periods. Like many young noblemen, he served as a page in his boyhood and as a courtier when he was a young man. He twice served briefly as a gentleman volunteer in military actions. During the second action he was severely wounded, and during his convalescence he reflected on his life and underwent a religious conversion. The second phase (1521–1540) comprised the pilgrim years when he traveled about Europe; he obtained an education, gathered like-minded companions, and tried various options as to how he might best serve God and other people. During the third phase, his last sixteen years, Loyola resided in Rome and served as superior general of the Jesuits. He devoted his time to prayer and some active ministry to people in need; his efforts, however, focused on organizing and directing the nascent Society of Jesus that was gradually spreading from Europe to Africa, Asia, and the Americas. The first forty-five years Loyola's biography can focus sharply on the man himself, but while he was a student at the University of Paris, he also gathered a group of companions who shared his ideals. The last twenty years of his life were so closely intermeshed with those of his Paris companions and later key recruits that his story cannot be studied in isolation from theirs.

The sixty-five years of Loyola's lifetime were a turbulent and creative era in Western history. His native Spain came together as a country and launched a colonial empire, events in which his own older brothers were deeply involved. The Europe of his adult life was dominated by four great rulers and repeated wars. Henry VIII (1509–1547) of England was the most colorful and least powerful. Francis I (1515–1547) of France was the epitome of the Renaissance prince: warrior, lover, and patron of art and literature. The most powerful was Suleiman the Magnificent (1520–1566), whose Ottoman Turkish empire stretched from Budapest to Baghdad, from Armenia to Algeria. The most important ruler for Loyola's own life was Charles V (1519–1556), Holy Roman Emperor, king of Spain, king of Naples, duke of Milan, ruler of the Netherlands, and lord over many other European principalities and vast colonial lands in North and South America. These rulers fought repeated wars, some of which profoundly affected Loyola's life. The main wars pitted Charles V against Suleiman and Francis I. Henry VIII sometimes played a secondary role. Warfare between Charles V and the Ottoman Empire went on for decades with only short lapses. Early in his career Suleiman conquered most of Hungary and besieged Vienna. Charles's army fought the Turks in the Balkans while his navy struggled for control of the western Mediterranean Sea and his army tried to establish bases in Tunisia and Algeria. Charles in person led an expedition that captured Tunis in 1535. Naval conflicts with the Turks forced Loyola to give up his own goal of spending his life in Jerusalem.

The two strongest Christian rulers were Francis I and Charles V; they fought four wars during Loyola's lifetime, plus another one between Charles V and Henry II (1547–1559) of France—these are called the **Habsburg-Valois Wars,** from the names of the royal dynasties involved. There were several reasons for these wars, notably rival claims to Milan and Naples. In the first of these wars Loyola was seriously wounded, and his life was changed profoundly.

As will be seen, these wars provided the political framework of Loyola's adult years. Their most important side effect was that Charles V, a strong Roman Catholic, had to devote his energy and resources to fending off the French and Turks and so could not intervene to stop the spread of Lutheranism in Germany until it had set down firm roots. In Germany, both Lutheran and Catholic princes and free cities had established alliance systems to protect themselves and their churches. The Lutheran alliance was called the **Schmalkaldic League.** In 1547, when Charles V enjoyed a truce with France and the Turks, he turned to Germany, where he made alliances with Catholics and with some pliant Lutheran princes. He then launched and won the First Schmalkaldic War. He set about trying to restore Catholicism in Germany, but failed. Lutheranism was firmly rooted in peoples' hearts, and the Emperor had neither enough soldiers nor priests to force Lutherans back to Catholicism. His effort ended abruptly in 1552, when the Lutheran princes made a secret alliance with Henry II of France and attacked and defeated the unsuspecting emperor in the Second Schmalkaldic War.

In the aftermath, Charles V abdicated and retired to a Spanish monastery. He resigned his lands in central Europe and his title of emperor to his brother Ferdinand, and the rest of his many lands went to his son Philip II. The Peace of Augsburg (1555), which ended the war, gave German princes and free cities the right to decide whether their official religion would be Catholic or Lutheran. The treaty brought a high degree of religious peace to Germany until the Thirty Years' Wars broke out in 1618. Loyola's Paris companions served as chaplains in the army of Charles fighting the Lutherans and in his navy fighting the Turks. Among Loyola's most interesting letters are one to Charles on how he should carry on his naval war against the Turks and another to Ferdinand on how he should deal with Lutherans in Austria.

The first chapter of this biography traces Loyola's early life as a nobleman and courtier from his birth in 1491 until a cannonball smashed his leg in 1521 and forced him to re-think his life. The next two chapters trace his religious conversion during his convalescence and his pilgrimage to Jerusalem. Chapters 4 and 5 examine his years (1524–1535) as a student at Barcelona, Alcalá, Salamanca, and Paris. The next two chapters relate how Loyola returned to Spain in 1535, then rejoined his student companions from his Paris years. War forced them to give up their dream of spending their lives in Jerusalem; instead they decided to start the Jesuit religious order, which received papal authorization in 1540. Chapter 8 studies the Spiritual Exercises, his great contribution to Christian spirituality.

The second half of this biography covers the last sixteen years of Loyola's life at Rome, when he was superior general of the Jesuit order. Here our account abandons a chronological framework; the chapters explore different aspect of Loyola's work. Chapter 9 relates missionary efforts of Loyola's companions in Ireland and Asia and glances at missions to Ethiopia and Brazil. Chapter 10 examines Loyola's own work as superior general of a growing religious order and his relationship with supporters. Chapter 11 covers the context and rhythms of Loyola's life at Rome and looks at his personal work on behalf of prostitutes, poor girls, down-on-their-luck nobles, and Jews who wanted to become Christians. The next two chapters trace his role in the growth of Jesuit schools and his work with women. Chapter 14 looks at the men who opposed his plans for the Jesuits; most of them were influential Catholic churchmen, but some were even Jesuits. Chapter 15 studies three important writings of his Roman years: his spiritual diary, his autobiography, and the Jesuit Constitutions. The last chapter traces his declining health, his death, and burial. A bibliographic essay serves as an appendix and gives an overview of the more than 2,000 books and articles about Loyola, his work, and his writings.

Europe, in the sixteenth century, experienced enormous religious change. Dynamic leaders, such as Martin Luther and John Calvin, founded Protestant churches that continue in Europe and the Americas till today. Most Europeans, however, remained loyal to Roman Catholicism, but the Catholic church, too, changed dramatically. Arguably, Ignatius of Loyola contributed more than anyone to reforming and refashioning Catholicism. Trained as a courtier, he was wounded in battle and underwent a religious conversion. He made working God's glory his goal in life, but for almost two decades he searched in Spain, Palestine, France, and Italy for the best way to attain his goal. In 1540, Loyola and the companions he had gathered at the University of Paris founded the Jesuit religious order. Loyola settled in Rome for the rest of his life, writing books and thousands of letters of advice and sending out his fellow Jesuits to preach and teach throughout Catholic Europe. During his last fifteen years, he also sent Jesuit missionaries to Brazil, Ethiopia, India, Indonesia, Malaysia, and Japan. Today there are more than 20,000 Jesuits in 106 countries and six continents carrying on Loyola's work.

Acknowledgments

Authors of books regularly run up many debts while working on a project, and I have incurred many while writing this short biography of Saint Ignatius of Loyola. Peter Stearns, provost at George Mason University, first invited me to contribute to this series and has given me both encouragement and sage advice since I accepted the project. I also owe a debt to Erika Gutierrez and Patrick McCarthy at Longman Publishers for their encouragement and editorial work. Eugene Merz, S.J., an expert on Ignatian spirituality here at Marquette University, went over the whole manuscript but was especially helpful with the chapter on Loyola's Spiritual Exercises. Robert Bireley, S.J., of Loyola University, who has published extensively on Jesuit activities during the Reformation, also went through the whole manuscript and made many suggestions for its improvement that I have followed. Jason Hostutler read the manuscript from a student's viewpoint and offered suggestions. I remain responsible for all mistakes. Thomas Caldwell and Richard Sherburne, both Jesuits at Marquette University, helped me with several computer problems. José Adolfo González, S.J., rector of the Collegio Internazionale del Gesù in Rome, gave me permission to print several illustrations. I was able to reprint all the illustrations in this book from *Ars Jesuitica* (St. Louis: Institute of Jesuit Sources, 2000) edited by Thomas Rochford, S.J., and J. J. Mueller, S.J., with their gracious permission. I am also grateful for the assistance of the librarians at Marquette University.

Saints, like monarchs, are usually called and listed in encyclopedias by their first name rather than their family name. Here I have alternated between both the family name (Loyola) and the first name (Iñigo, later changed to Ignatius), largely for the sake of variety.

John Patrick Donnelly

The Early Years of a Basque Nobleman

The full name of Ignatius of Loyola was originally *Iñigo López de Oñaz y Loyola*. The names of the family estates, *Oñaz* and *Loyola*, became in effect the family name. Here we will call him Iñigo until he arrives at the **University of Paris**, where his first name was changed to *Ignatius*, a name more familiar to non-Spaniards. **Castle Loyola**, where Iñigo was born, still stands in a valley of the Basque country of northern Spain near the French border, on the edge of the Pyrenees mountains. The valley, rich in apple and chestnut trees, was overshadowed by Mount Izarraitz, from which the Bay of Biscay and the Atlantic Ocean could be seen on clear days.

Records of Iñigo's family's noble status go back to the late twelfth century, and his family's wealth in his lifetime has been estimated at more than 80,000 ducats, a very considerable sum. Iñigo was born sometime in 1491, but no exact records survive. Little is known of his mother, Marina Sánchez de Licona. His father, Beltrán (c. 1439–1507), had fought on the side of King Ferdinand of Aragon and Queen Isabella of Castile in the civil war that brought them to power against other claimants to the throne of Castile. Their marriage was crucial in joining disparate kingdoms of medieval Iberia into modern Spain. The monarchs rewarded Beltrán with praise and the right of patronage over the church of **Azpeitia,** the town nearest to Castle Loyola. The patronage rights allowed Beltrán and his successors to name the pastor and his assistants and to claim most of the parish revenue. Many noblemen had similar claims on local churches.

Iñigo was the youngest of thirteen children born to Beltrán. Iñigo never had much contact with his mother, who may have died shortly after his birth. Consequently he was turned over to a wet-nurse, María Garín, and spent his first years in her modest home rather than his father's nearby castle. From her Iñigo learned to speak Basque rather than Castilian (or Spanish, as it is called today). Only after Iñigo moved from his native province of Guipúzcoa to serve at court did his Castilian improve, and he never achieved full fluency. Most of the people in Azpeitia were **Basques,** a unique people who seem to have inhabited the valleys of northern Spain many centuries before Celtic tribes migrated across the Pyrenees mountains and occupied most of Spain almost 4,000 years ago. Later the Romans conquered Spain and imposed their Latin language, which gradually developed into Spanish during the Middle Ages. Today there are about a million Basques, mostly in Spain but some in southern France and the Americas. Many Spanish Basques still long for their own national state. The Basque language is related to no other language on the face of the earth. Basques tend to be taller than other Spaniards, but Iñigo himself was of short stature, at most five feet, four inches tall.

Biographers interested in psychological history have speculated on how the lack of contact with his mother influenced his development and personality. Iñigo had six older brothers and three sisters, plus an illegitimate half brother and two illegitimate half sisters. Little is known about his illegitimate siblings. His oldest brother, Juan, commanded a ship and later fought on land in the Spanish army under Gonzalo de Córdoba, known as "el Gran Capitán," who took over control of the Kingdom of Naples from the French. Juan died at Naples shortly after the decisive Battle of Atella in 1506. Another brother, Beltrán, also fought and died in Naples. A third brother, Ochoa, served as a soldier in Spain and the Netherlands, while Hernando went to the Americas in 1510 and seems to have died in Central America fighting Indians. The second youngest brother, Pero, became a priest and eventually served as pastor of the local church at Azpeitia, where he earned a reputation for dissolute living. On the death of Juan in Naples, Martín García, as the oldest living brother, became heir to most of his parents' rights and property. He took over as head of the family on his father's death in 1507. Iñigo's three full sisters married husbands from the lower nobility.

Young Iñigo of Loyola was born in 1491, on the eve of Spain's Golden Age. The marriage of Ferdinand and Isabella in 1469 had joined Aragon and Castile, but each kingdom retained its own parliament and laws. In 1492 their united armies completed the conquest of Granada, the last Muslim foothold in southern Spain. The fall of Granada freed money for Isabella to finance the project of Christopher Columbus to open a trade route to India and China by sailing westward across the Atlantic. Most contemporary experts considered it a harebrained proposal, not because they thought the earth was flat but because they rightly thought the earth was far larger than did Columbus. They were right. Columbus never came near China; instead he opened the Americas to Spanish exploration, colonization, and exploitation.

As we have seen, one of Loyola's brothers joined those overseas adventures. Within a short time, Spain became a world power. The campaigning of el Gran Capitán in Naples laid the foundation of two centuries of Spanish domination of Italy and earned for Spanish soldiers the reputation of being the finest in Europe. Finally, Ferdinand also conquered and annexed most of the Kingdom of Navarre, along the Spanish-French border, in 1512. Iñigo's oldest living brother, Martín García, fought in this campaign. All these lands became part of a much larger empire of **Charles V** when Ferdinand died in 1516. Charles already controlled the old Burgundian lands, most notably the Netherlands, and the Habsburg lands in central Europe. In 1519 he was elected Holy Roman Emperor. No European ruler between Charlemagne and Napoleon held such vast possessions—or had so many enemies to deal with: the French, the Turks, and the Lutherans of Germany. Later Cortés and Pizzaro added Mexico and Peru to his domains. Charles V abdicated and retired to a monastery in 1556, the year of Loyola's death. His long reign shaped the political world in which Loyola lived and worked.

All these conquests and acquisitions presented the Spanish monarchs with problems; for rulers in their age, diversity, particularly religious diversity, meant weakness. To unify their realms religiously, Ferdinand and Isabella persuaded Pope Sixtus IV in 1478 to set up the Spanish **Inquisition,** over which the Spanish crown held control. The main goal of the Inquisition was to force Spanish Jews and Muslims who had accepted baptism to believe and live as orthodox Christians. Spain had the largest Muslim and Jewish minorities anywhere in Europe outside the Balkans. Gradually pressure on Muslims to convert was increased. Then in 1492 Ferdinand and Isabella issued a decree that all Jews must either accept baptism or leave Spain. Once Jews and Muslims were baptized, they fell under the jurisdiction of the Inquisition. Many Jews accepted Christianity nominally to prevent their expulsion but continued to believe and practice their ancestral religion in their hearts and homes. The bloodiest persecution in the history of the Inquisition was under Ferdinand and Isabella and fell mainly on Jews. Repeatedly Iñigo Loyola would also fall under the Inquisition's suspicion, even though Basques were ardent supporters of Catholicism.

What career choices faced the younger sons of the middle-level nobility? A business career would have tainted the family reputation. Basically there were three choices: the military, the church, or the court. Initially Iñigo's father steered him toward a church career. While still a young lad, he was tonsured as a cleric, but when he seemed to show little interest in becoming a priest, his father sent him to court as a page. Sometime between 1504 and 1507 Juan Velázquez de Cuéllar, chief treasurer of Castile and one of Spain's most distinguished noblemen, had written Iñigo's father, Don Beltrán, suggesting that one of his sons be brought up as a page in his household. Serving as a page at noble courts was common for the sons of the lesser nobility. It would open a career as a courtier, that is, a court gentleman who served in any task to which he was assigned: sometimes as an administrator, sometimes as a gentleman volunteer or part-time warrior, sometimes simply as an ornamental court butterfly. This was an opportunity to be seized. Don Beltrán sent Iñigo off to Velázquez's court at Arévalo, in central Castile, where he served until Velázquez's death in 1517. There was a royal palace at Arévalo where King Ferdinand stayed periodically in 1508, 1510, 1511, and 1515, but Ferdinand's court moved about, and therefore Velázquez had to move about with his master. The royal court visited Valladolid, Burgos, Tordesillas, Madrid, Segovia, and Cordoba during the period 1506–1515. Young Iñigo likely accompanied his master on these travels, and he almost certainly met King Ferdinand several times.

Gradually Iñigo's Spanish improved, and he developed a superb penmanship. He wrote some poetry, cultivated a lasting taste for music, learned to play the lute, and acquired the courtly manners of a gentleman. Years later his secretary, Juan Polanco, described him as "the most courteous and polite of men." Velázquez had six sons, and very likely Iñigo found most of his recreation riding and hunting with them. His reading during this period of his life seems to have been mainly romances of chivalry, a popular literary genre among the nobility. Prince Ferdinand, the younger brother of Charles V, also lived at the court in Arévalo. When Charles abdicated in 1556, Ferdinand became Holy Roman Emperor and was the real founder of the Austrian Habsburg dynasty, which ruled much of east central Europe until 1918. Late in life Loyola sent him an important letter of advice on how to foster Catholicism in his lands.

Many years later Juan Polanco wrote that, during his years at Arévalo, Iñigo was attached to the Catholic faith but did not live up to its ideals and was "careless about gambling, affairs with women, brawls and the use of arms." In his autobiography, written late in life, Loyola tells us that he was enormously attracted to a woman at court whose status was higher than that of a countess or duchess. Two possible objects of his infatuation have been suggested, both sisters of Charles V: one was Princess Leonor of Austria, whom he might often have seen at Valladolid; a second possibility was her beautiful sister Catalina of Austria, who was later queen of Portugal. He may have met her once or twice. Loyola had no possibility of marrying a woman of such lofty status. Some scholars think that the woman of his dreams was exactly that, and not a real person. In mentioning his youthful infatuation, they contend, Iñigo was looking back not with nostalgia but with amusement—he was dreaming impossible dreams, whether they dealt with an idealized romance or daring deeds of knightly valor. The romances of chivalry that were his favorite reading fostered such fantasies.

We know little about Loyola's life as a courtier, but one nasty incident stands out, largely because it gave rise to a court case. In 1515 he returned to his hometown of Azpeitia to celebrate Mardi Gras; he and his priest brother were involved in a premeditated brawl in the dark of night. Precisely what happened is not clear. Was it a quarrel over a woman? It seems that a deliberate plot was set up to assault somebody and that Iñigo was the ringleader. There is no way to know, but the affair was serious enough to attract the attention of the governor of the province of Guipúzcoa. To protect himself from punishment Iñigo fled to **Pamplona,** the provincial capital, to seek the bishop's protection on the grounds that he had been tonsured and therefore enjoyed the right of a cleric to be tried before a church court, which was more likely to be lenient than a civil court. He was in fact arrested and confined to the episcopal prison. The governor understandably rejected his claim of clerical status—Loyola had never worn clerical garb but had dressed as a court gentleman with cape, a red cap and sword, and shoulder-length blond hair. Often he even went about wearing a breastplate. Eventually Iñigo was able to get back to Arévalo, but the affair could well have crushed any future as a courtier. Almost certainly his noble status and his connections with important people saved him from conviction as a criminal.

Within a year Iñigo's prospects as a courtier nearly crashed for reasons over which he had no control. His patron, Juan Velázquez, disagreed with the policy of the new king, Charles V, and fell from favor shortly before his death in August 1517. Partly with the help of Velázquez's widow, Iñigo was able to find a new patron in the duke of Nájera, who accepted him as a gentleman and courtier in his household. Nájera was viceroy of Navarre, which King

Ferdinand had conquered five years earlier. Very likely Iñigo accompanied his new master to Valladolid when Charles V officially took office as King of Castile in February of 1518. Many towns of Castile did not favor this young king, who had been brought up in the Netherlands and was regarded as an outsider surrounded by foreign advisors; furthermore, Charles seemed a threat to the cherished liberties of the Castilian towns. A wave of riots swept Castile, and the town of Nájera rose up against its Duke. He responded by organizing a minor expedition that quelled the rebellion in September of 1518. Iñigo served very briefly as a gentleman volunteer in that expedition, his first military service. More serious was the Revolt of the Comuneros (a coalition of cities to protect their traditional rights) in 1521, which spread from the towns of Castile to Loyola's home province of Guipúzcoa and to Azpeitia. Charles V was absent from Spain, so the Council of Castile entered negotiations with the rebels. While Nájera prepared his soldiery, he also sent a team of negotiators to Guipúzcoa. Since Iñigo was a native of the region, he was almost certainly one of the negotiators. The towns agreed to submit to a compromise worked out by Nájera in April 1521.

This was but a minor incident in a much greater problem. The absence of Charles V from Spain and the revolt of the Comuneros (or towns) presented Francis I, king of France, with a marvelous opportunity to invade Spain and support the claims of Henri d'Albert to the crown of Navarre. He was confident that many Navarrese would support his plans. A French army of 12,000 infantry, a strong contingent of cavalry, and twenty-nine cannons invaded Spain on 12 May 1521; they soon took up a position a mile from Pamplona, the capital of Guipúzcoa. Nájera sent 1,000 soldiers under the command of Francés de Beaumont to defend the city. Meanwhile Iñigo and his brother Martín García brought up some reinforcements they had raised in Guipúzcoa. The townspeople, however, thought differently—why have their town destroyed to defend the rights of Charles V, that absent Dutchman? After a quarrel with the townspeople, Beaumont decided to evacuate the city, whose fortifications were old and no match for the French artillery. Martín García agreed with Beaumont. Iñigo, however, and the local governor decided to make a last-ditch defense of the citadel. But on May 19 the town officials swore fealty to the French claimant, Henri d'Albert, and the French army began its assault on the citadel. The next day Iñigo was struck by a small cannon ball that smashed his legs; his right leg was shattered and the left was wounded. The citadel surrendered on May 24.

The wound forever changed Loyola's life, as we shall see. He served as a gentleman volunteer, not as a soldier, for perhaps ten days in all, including both the uprising at Nájera in 1520 and the battle at Pamplona in 1521. Hundreds of books speak of Loyola as the soldier saint and characterize not only his own life but also that of the Jesuits he founded by catchphrases such as "soldiers of Christ" or "shock troops of the papacy." These phrases have little historical basis.

Why did Loyola, who later in life showed himself a man of keen practical judgment, lead the nearly hopeless defense of Pamplona? Why did he not retreat with his brother and the other men who had come from Guipúzcoa? He suggested the reason in his autobiography. His early life was built on ambition, vainglory, dreams of chivalry, and the hope that deeds of daring would enhance his career as a courtier. If he died defending Pamplona, he would die gloriously. Iñigo was never a man for half measures. He certainly remembered that his father, Beltrán, had won glory fighting against an earlier French invasion. Not far from Pamplona lay the valley of Roncesvalles, where Roland, the most famous knight of medieval French literature, had met a heroic death in 778.

Loyola is wounded at the Battle of Pamplona.

Renaissance authors continued to glorify Roland; two of Italy's greatest writers, Matteo Maria Boiardo and Lodovico Ariosto, published long epic poems glorifying Roland in the decades just before the Battle of Pamplona.

The French at Pamplona, it seems, were impressed by Loyola's gallantry and gave him medical treatment. They also assigned some captured soldiers to carry him back to Castle Loyola. When they got him home, his family discovered that his legs were not healing, either because they were badly set or had been displaced by the rocking of his litter on the trip home. Local doctors would have to reset his right leg. There were, of course, no anesthetics, and the pain was excruciating. But Loyola, true to his knightly code, gave no sign of pain except for clenching his fists. After the operation his health declined to the point that the doctors told him to go to confession because he would die if he did not improve by midnight. But improve he did, and rapidly. He attributed his recovery to the intervention of St. Peter.

Then a new problem arose. The doctors had set his bones badly. His right leg was noticeably shorter than his left, so that he limped. Worse, a portion of bone protruded on his right leg, so that he would be disfigured for life. In the Renaissance, women's legs were never seen in public, but gentlemen wore tight leggings from their shoes to the top of their thighs so they could show off handsome legs. Iñigo asked his doctors if the protruding bone could be cut away; they replied that it could, but only with excruciating pain. He ordered them to carry out the operation. Again, his autobiography looks back on this as a sign not only of his determination but of his vanity and worldly thirst to cut a glamorous figure in court circles, regardless of the price.

Iñigo now faced a convalescence that lasted nine months. Although his basic health returned quickly, he could not put weight on his right leg, so he had to spend most of his time reclining in bed. To relieve his boredom, he asked for books on chivalry. His favorite reading had been *Amadís de Gaul* by García Ordóñez de Montalvo, published in 1500. This book glorified knights who yearned for romance with beautiful but unattainable women. No such books were to be found in Castle Loyola. Since only Books of piety were available, reluctantly, Iñigo began to read them. They changed his life and indirectly influenced hundreds of thousands of people over the next five centuries.

The Conversion
of a Courtier

During his recovery, Loyola's family brought him two large books to read. One was *The Life of our Lord Jesus Christ from the Four Gospels* by Ludolf of Saxony in four hefty volumes, which had recently been published in a Spanish translation. Ludolf (c. 1295–1377) was a Carthusian monk who embellished the accounts of the original gospels with extracts from the early Church Fathers and medieval spiritual writers. The second book was a collected lives of the saints known as *The Golden Legend*, written by Jacopo da Varazze (c. 1230–1298), archbishop of Genoa. Jacopo's book was enormously popular and had run through more than a hundred editions in many languages by 1500. Its purpose was to edify rather than to give an accurate account of the saints' lives. Loyola found it more fascinating than Ludolf's more sober volumes. His autobiography indicates how attractive he found the lives of the saints but also how his delight in their deeds was immature and vainglorious. What he found attractive in the saints was not the love of God and neighbor or deep prayer but rather striking acts of religious valor, such as severe penances or stringent fasting. Thus, while he found attractive the lives of Saint Dominic and Saint Francis of

Assisi, both well-known as the founders of the Dominicans and Franciscans, he was particularly fascinated by the bizarre Saint Humphrey, who spent seventy years completely alone in the Egyptian desert eating dates; he was clothed only by a belt of leaves and by his long hair, which fell to his ankles so that he looked like a wild animal. Loyola's reading inspired him to imitate the saints. As he said in his autobiography, "St. Francis did this, so I must do it; St. Dominic did this, so I must do it." He determined that he had to keep a record of what most impressed him in his readings, so he secured a large notebook of some six hundred pages and began writing down extracts in his own skilled hand. He even used several kinds of ink; thus he recorded the words of Christ in red, those of the Virgin Mary in blue, and the rest of his notes in black ink. Unfortunately, his notebook has not survived.

More important than the readings themselves were his ruminations over them. After reflecting on performing mighty deeds in God's service, he returned to thoughts of knightly valor, particularly those done to impress the woman of his dreams. Gradually he recognized that in the aftermath of his dreams of valor he felt dry and discontented; in contrast, his meditations about serving God, going to Jerusalem, living on herbs, or rivaling the saints in acts of penance left him consoled and content. He decided that the first set of daydreams were inspired by the devil and the second by God. He also saw that his past life was sinful so that he needed to do penance for it, and he determined to make a pilgrimage to Jerusalem. Lying awake one night, he was convinced that Mary with the infant Jesus had visited and consoled him, and he claimed that after this experience he no longer experienced the sexual temptations of his youth.

Iñigo's religious conversion did not go unnoticed by his family. His brother Martín García took him aside one day, led him through the rooms of the castle, told him how people had high hopes for him and warned against throwing away his career. Iñigo gave his brother an ambiguous reply and planned to slip away on his projected pilgrimage. He told his brother that he was planning to visit the duke of Nájera, his old patron. Meanwhile he felt that, after he returned from Jerusalem, he would probably join the Carthusians, the most austere of the Catholic religious orders. He even asked a servant who was going to Burgos to gather information there for him about the Carthusians and their lifestyle.

In February 1522 Iñigo and his priest-brother, Pero set out for Oñate; there he left his brother and headed on for the famous shrine of the Black Madonna at Montserrat. He rode a donkey, both because he was still wearing the clothes of a gentleman and because his bad leg prevented much walking. Even though he was riding, his foot was always swollen by nightfall. On the way he visited his sister Magdalena to wish her farewell. He then pushed on to Navarrete to see the duke of Nájera, whose household owed him some ducats. The duke had fallen from favor, had been dismissed as viceroy of Navarre, and was suffering financial difficulties; nevertheless he insisted on paying Iñigo, who then returned part of the money and asked that some of it be used to pay some debts Iñigo owed, presumably to servants in the Duke's household. The rest he earmarked for the restoration of a local image of the Virgin. When Loyola looked back on his piety in these days, he remembered his enthusiasm and sincere repentance for past sins, but he was also aware of how he ignored virtues such as humility, patience, and charity and how he was fixated on performing severe physical penances.

His autobiography illustrates his spiritual naivete by recalling an incident that occurred while he was riding his mule from Navarrete toward Montserrat. He caught up with a **Moor.** They conversed and soon started discussing the virginity of Mary, the mother of Jesus. The Moor agreed that Mary had conceived as a virgin but averred that the birth of her child had stripped her of virginity. They argued the point, and the Moor pushed on ahead. Iñigo gradually became more incensed over what he considered the Moor's blasphemy. He debated seriously about whether he should uphold Mary's honor by riding up to the Moor and stabbing him to death. Scruples arose. Sighting a fork in the road ahead, he decided to let slack the reins on his mule: if the mule followed the broader road, which the Moor had taken, Iñigo would kill him. Fortunately the mule followed the narrow road heading toward Montserrat.

Why did Loyola relate his encounter with the Moor in his autobiography? Only he would have known of it, and it was certainly embarrassing. He tells us why just before relating the encounter: "Along the road something happened that is worth noting because it helps us understand how God dealt with this soul. For all his great desire for serving God in so far as he could understand it, he was still blind. He determined to do great penances. . . . When he decided to do a penance done by the saints, he set himself to do that much and much more." His zeal and generosity lacked wisdom and moderation. In exposing his own lack of balance and wisdom in the encounter with the Moor, he hoped to teach his followers that headstrong zeal and a thirst for glory can easily lead to atrocities and shame.

Shortly before reaching the shrine at Montserrat, which is still a major pilgrimage site, Iñigo stopped in a town and prepared to hide his identity. He bought some rough cloth usually used for making sacks and had a tailor fashion a rude cloak falling down to his feet. He planned to wear the cloak on his pilgrimage to Jerusalem. He also bought a sandal made of hemp for his sore and swollen foot. To these he added a walking staff and a gourd for carrying water. He carefully prepared a written account of his sins, which he went over with a confessor for three days. This enormously long confession was most unusual—clearly Iñigo wanted to put his past completely behind him and start a new life with a clean slate. It did not prove so easy. On March 25, the evening after the confession, he went to the famous shrine of Mary and made an all-night vigil, kneeling and standing, locked in prayer. He arranged for his confessor to hang his sword and dagger in the church as a votive offering. This was a ritual he had read about in the story of the great knight Amadis of Gaul. The next day he secretly gave his fine clothes to a local beggar and set off for **Barcelona,** but he avoided the main road, where he might run into the entourage of the recently elected Pope Hadrian VI. He feared someone in the pope's entourage might recognize him; the new pope was Adrian of Utrecht, the pious former tutor of Charles V. Three miles from Montserrat a man rushed up to him and asked if he had given his clothes to a beggar. He said he had, and saved the beggar from punishment for theft.

Some miles farther down the road was the small town of Manresa. Iñigo decided to stop there for a few days so he could add some recent reflections to his notebook. The few days grew into almost eleven months. Three converging factors delayed his pilgrimage. First, the spread of plague caused the authorities at Barcelona to keep outsiders from entering their city. That meant that Iñigo had to postpone his plans to sail from Barcelona to Rome, where he could obtain the required papal authorization to join a pilgrimage to Jerusalem. Second, that delay meant he would miss the annual pilgrimage ship scheduled to sail from Venice. Third and perhaps most important, at Manresa Iñigo began to undergo a series of religious experiences that changed him radically.

At Manresa he stayed initially at a hospice that served the sick and indigent, but he soon moved to a room the local Dominican friars made available to him in their convent. He started to help poor and sick people and began to build up a circle of friends. The most important was a Dominican priest, Galcerán Perelló, who became his confessor. Iñigo had a remarkable ability to make friends and enlist support for his projects, and he did this at Manresa despite wandering about in his long sackcloth gown, not cutting his nails, and not combing or cutting his hair. His friends took him in when he fell ill and gave him alms to live on. Six days a week he fasted, avoiding meat and wine. Most of his time was spent in prayer in a hillside cave overlooking the Cardoner River, which ran through the town.

Iñigo soon gained the nickname "the holy man." He went around engaging people in spiritual conversations, sometimes giving advice, sometimes seeking it. He especially valued conversations with an elderly woman whose reputation for holiness was so great that King Ferdinand had sought her advice.

Iñigo probably returned periodically to Montserrat to get advice from the French monk Jean Chanon, to whom he had made his exhaustive confession. Chanon provided him with a copy of *The Imitation of Christ,* by the Belgian Thomas à Kempis (1380–1471), the most popular spiritual book of the fifteenth century. Iñigo prized it above all nonbiblical writings, and for centuries it was required reading for Jesuit novices. Chanon may have also given him a copy of the *Ejercitatorio de la Vida Espiritual* (Exercises for the Spiritual Life), written by the former abbot of Montserrat, García Jiménez de Cisneros, and published at the monastery in 1500. From it Iñigo could have learned techniques of systematic meditation. Despite their similar titles and subject matter, it is hard to trace specific influences of Jiménez's book on Loyola's own later masterpiece, the **Spiritual Exercises.** Iñigo devoted seven hours each day in his room at the Dominican convent or in his cave to prayer, plus attending daily **Mass.** He also joined the Dominicans when they chanted their evening prayers.

It is not clear whether he had a copy of the Bible or New Testament at Manresa. He does tell us that he used to read the passion of Christ while attending mass.

The eleven months Iñigo spent at Manresa were the most turbulent of his whole life. After several months of peaceful spiritual development, he encountered a period of crisis. First, he began to have doubts whether he could sustain his new life for many decades to come. He decided that this was a temptation from the devil and scornfully replied to the devil, "Can you promise me even a single hour of life?" That temptation disappeared, only to be followed by a worse crisis. Had he really confessed all his sins to Chanon at Montserrat? Again and again he went to confession, trying to remember all his youthful sins so that he might find peace and be assured of forgiveness. During this struggle he kept up his prayer and shouted to God for help. "If I thought I could find a cure, no struggle would be too hard for me. Even if I have to follow around a puppy dog for it to give me a cure, I will do it." But peace did not come. He seriously considered committing suicide, but he thought that would be sinful. Instead he decided on a total fast, no food or drink, until God delivered him from his scruples or he came to the brink of death. Fortunately after a week of this he went to confession and told the priest what he was doing. The confessor ordered him to stop the fast, and for a couple of days he was free of scruples. Then they came back. He was tempted to return to his life as a court gentleman, but at this point he recognized he must stop going back over his old confessions and must cling to the conviction that God's mercy had liberated him. At that his scruples finally disappeared.

Iñigo's last months at Manresa were filled with inward consolation. He had few responsibilities, and his relationship with God now entered a new, higher, mystical level, which filled him with joy. In his autobiography he tells us that God was now teaching him like a schoolmaster does a pupil. He began to have what might be called visions, but they were not so much seen as experienced. For instance, he long had been devoted to the Holy Trinity, the traditional Christian belief that the one God exists as a threefold reality of Father, Son, and Holy Spirit sharing one intellect and one will. His "vision" of the Trinity was of three musical keys, different but in harmony. This experience brought him enormous consolation and tears of joy. One day at mass, he tells us, he experienced the risen Christ, but neither big nor small and without distinct limbs. He claims to have had a similar experience of the Virgin Mary, again without distinct parts. Once he was going to church, walking above the bank of the Cardoner River; he sat down and was enlightened about spiritual things, matters of both faith and learning, "not that he saw some vision." In his autobiography he claimed that all his later religious experiences and his university training taught him less than that one experience. That same day he had another experience of an object of surpassing beauty, but he recognized it as the work of the devil and spurned it. He also began to eat meat, abandoned his unkempt appearance, and returned to cutting his nails and hair.

While at Manresa Iñigo continued to compile notes that later evolved into one of the most influential spiritual books in history, published in 1548 as *The Spiritual Exercises*. Shortly after his return from Jerusalem in 1523 he was directing people through the Spiritual Exercises, and we know that handwritten copies of the book then existed that he kept revising. The Exercises tried to help devout men and women share what Iñigo had experienced at Manresa.

During December of 1522, Iñigo's last month at Manresa, he fell seriously ill. An upper-class family moved him to their home, and several prominent women cared for him around the clock. He slowly recovered but continued to have stomach pains for the rest of his life. His poor health almost certainly stemmed in part from the extreme austerities he practiced at Manresa; later in life he discouraged his followers from such penances because they could hurt their ability to work for God and their neighbors.

Concerned for his health, the women provided him with warm clothes, including a sort of beret and two plain coats of heavy cloth. Among the women at Manresa he probably touched the heart of the widow Inés Pascal the most. She met him when he first arrived at Manresa, directed him to the hospice, and invited him to join her family for supper. He made such an impression that fifty years later her son remembered what they ate that night: broth and chicken. Loyola's earliest extant letter was written to her in 1524; in it he consoled her over the death of a woman friend and gave her spiritual advice. Indeed, a striking proportion of his early correspondence was spiritual counsel for women.

III

From Barcelona to Jerusalem and Back

While reading the life of Christ during his convalescence at Castle Loyola, Iñigo developed a romantic dream that dominated his life until 1537: he would go to Jerusalem, live near the sites of Christ's last days, and try to convert people there to Christianity. The same dream had dominated young Saint Francis of Assisi, who founded the Franciscans in the thirteenth century. A whole chapter of his rule for the Franciscan Order gave directives for friars who were making a pilgrimage to the Holy Land. Early in 1523 Iñigo left Manresa for Barcelona, the most important Spanish port on the Mediterranean Sea, so that he could find a ship to take him to Rome. At Easter time pilgrims traditionally came to Rome and obtained the Pope's authorization for a pilgrimage to Palestine.

Inés Pascal, who had befriended Iñigo at Manresa, owned a shop and home at Barcelona. He stayed there as her guest for some twenty days while he arranged details of his passage to Rome. Eager to share his religious enthusiasm with the people of the bustling port, he visited convents of monks and nuns. One day as he spoke to a cluster of children on the steps of a church, Isabel Roser spotted him, listened, and was struck by his personality. She and

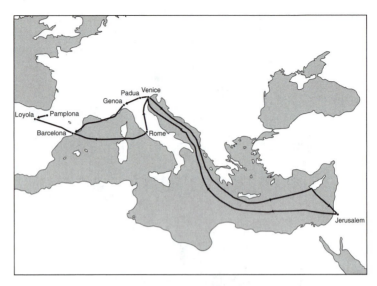

After recovering from his wounds in 1523, Loyola sailed from
Barcelona to Rome, crossed Italy to Venice, and took the annual pil-
grim ship from Venice to Jerusalem and back. He then returned to
Barcelona and began his studies.

her wealthy husband invited him to dinner, where he
spoke about the things of God. For the next decade Isabel
became his most important benefactor and later tried and
failed to found an order of women Jesuits.

Loyola did not want to travel to Palestine the easy way,
gathering a full purse of alms from benefactors and joining companions bound for Jerusalem. Rather he wanted
to go alone and without financial resources as far as possible so that he would trust only in God's mercy. He feared
that, with companions, he might put his trust in them, not
God. He found a ship's captain who would give him free
passage but warned him to bring his own food. Then he
began to worry: would not taking food along on the ship
compromise total trust in God? Unable to decide, he put
the question to a confessor who used common sense and

told him to beg for food and bring it aboard. Iñigo accepted his advice. His ship sailed and enjoyed favorable winds, landing near Rome about 26 March 1523. Iñigo joined a woman and her daughter and son in walking to Rome. At a hostel, some soldiers provided them with food and drink. The woman and her daughter then went to an upstairs room to sleep, while Iñigo and her son slept in a nearby stable. He was awakened in the night by screams: the soldiers were about to rape the two women. He rushed to the scene, and his anger induced the soldiers to back away, though they could just as easily have killed him. Gathering the women and girl, Iñigo led them toward Rome in the middle of the night until they reached the town of Fondi. The gates were locked, and they had to await the dawn. That day, the woman and her daughter went on to Rome. He spent three days at Fondi, then walked on to Rome, where on March 31 he secured Hadrian VI's permission to visit the pilgrimage sites in Jerusalem.

The next week was **Holy Week,** which he spent in Rome before crossing Italy to the Adriatic Sea. He then headed north and in mid-May arrived at Venice, where he had to stay until his ship sailed on July 14. Initially he begged his bread and slept on the ground in the piazza in front of the magnificent Church of St. Mark. One day he so impressed a Spanish nobleman that the man offered Iñigo a room in his home until his departure. Getting passage was not easy, for he had no money, trusting in God's help. The Spanish ambassador secured him an audience with the Venetian doge, who was so struck by his sincerity that he ordered a Venetian ship heading to Cyprus on government business to give him free passage.

The number of pilgrims in 1523 was small. The Ottoman Turks had conquered Palestine in 1517 and added Rhodes in 1522. For the sake of their trade in the Middle East, the Venetians tried to maintain good relations with

Suleiman the Magnificent, the greatest of all the Turkish sultans, but the peace was uneasy. Only twenty-one pilgrims went to the Holy Land that year; among them were four Spaniards. The trip was expensive, and treatment from Turks and Arabs could be harsh. Iñigo brought no money. He was running a high fever when the ship was about to sail; a doctor told him that, if he boarded the ship, he would likely be buried at sea. He boarded anyway, and after a full month at sea he and the other pilgrims reached the island of Cyprus, a Venetian possession. There they had a five-day layover, followed by six days' sailing from Cyprus to Palestine; then the pilgrims languished in harbor at Joppa for another week before being allowed to disembark. It took two more days' riding on donkeys before the pilgrims, spotting Jerusalem from afar, broke off their conversation and commenced the last two miles with hearts filled with joy and prayer.

Several Franciscans met them at the city gate and led them into Jerusalem, carrying aloft a cross. There the pilgrims sought out the traditional holy places, visiting Mount Zion, the upper room where Jesus celebrated the Last Supper, and the Holy Sepulcher, his burial place, where they spent the whole night in prayer. The next afternoon they traced the traditional path on which Jesus carried the cross from the headquarters of Pontius Pilate to Mount Calvary, where he was crucified. The following days included visits to Bethany, the Mount of Olives, Bethlehem, and the Garden of Gethsemane, where Jesus prayed the night before his death. They also visited Jericho, the Jordan River, and other places traditionally associated with the life of Christ, but they did not go north to Galilee. Turkish troops guarded and hustled them along on these trips. Iñigo was profoundly moved by these experiences, and his plan to spend his life constantly revisiting the holy sites and trying to help souls became a fixed decision. The official pilgrimage ran from 4 to 22 September 1523.

As the other pilgrims were preparing to return home, Iñigo visited the Franciscan superior at Mount Zion and revealed his plan. The Franciscans had authority from the pope and the Turkish sultan to supervise pilgrims from Catholic Europe. After examining the letters of recommendation Iñigo carried, the superior told him that the Franciscans had barely enough food to feed themselves. Iñigo said that made no difference—he would need no help, aside from priests to hear his confession. The superior tried to discourage him, but the final decision was in the hands of the Franciscan provincial superior, who would be returning shortly from a visit to Bethlehem. Iñigo took heart and wrote farewell letters to friends, saying that he would spend his life in Jerusalem. It was not to be. The Franciscan provincial had heard similar plans before from pilgrims and pointed out to Iñigo that the Turks had killed or enslaved most of them. Iñigo said he would run the risk. The provincial then replied that he must leave with the other pilgrims or be excommunicated. When he started to show Loyola the papal documents giving him the power to excommunicate, Iñigo stopped him and agreed to return to Europe since he felt God was speaking through his official representative.

Iñigo had a vivid imagination and wanted to know and remember every concrete detail he could about the life of Jesus. As the other pilgrims were preparing to leave, he felt a keen desire to revisit the Mount of Olives, the traditional site of Christ's ascension into heaven. He sneaked out alone and, bribing the guards with his penknife, entered the site. After leaving he suddenly remembered that he had not checked the direction of the indentations attributed to the feet of Jesus. In what direction were the feet of Jesus pointing on the rock when he ascended into heaven? Iñigo returned and bribed the guards again with a little pair of scissors. (The supposed rock is still there, but the imprints are now worn away by the kisses of pilgrims over the centuries.) Meanwhile, the Franciscans could not find Iñigo and sent a servant to find him. Grabbing his arm and threatening him with a cane, the servant brought Iñigo back to the convent. Iñigo felt that Christ was with him in a special way while he was being pulled through the Jerusalem streets.

Late on September 23 the pilgrims headed toward the Mediterranean coast; they stopped at a town where the Turkish commander demanded a large bribe and detained them for a week. The voyage from Joppa to Cyprus took eleven days, during which several pilgrims fell sick and one died. Finding a ship from Cyprus to Venice proved difficult. The pilgrims split up, taking three different ships. Iñigo went on the smallest, which made it through storms to southern Italy after almost two months of sailing. The other two ships went down, one with all hands. It was two more weeks before Iñigo, clothed only in knee britches, a ragged shirt, and a light coat, reached Venice in mid-January. His Spanish friend in Venice took him in again and gave him some cloth and a few coins, which Iñigo gave to beggars. He would rely on God and the generosity of people he encountered for food. He folded the cloth across his stomach to ward off the bitter cold and started walking across northern Italy from Venice to Genoa, where he hoped to catch a ship to Barcelona.

He was fortunate to make it to Spain. Emperor Charles V, who was also king of Spain, was once more at war with Francis I of France. Most of the fighting was for possession of Milan, in northern Italy. Iñigo met some Spanish troops who advised him to skirt the contested area, but stubbornly trusting in God, he ignored them and soon ran into more Spanish soldiers, who arrested him as a spy and searched all his clothes. Finding no evidence, they led him to their commander. Iñigo, again, identifying with Jesus when he was on trial before Pilate and was carrying his cross, determined that he would not address the commander with the usual terms and signs of respect. When Iñigo would not doff his cap or address him with respect, the commander concluded that he was no spy but a madman or simpleton and let him go.

The next afternoon Iñigo was arrested by French soldiers, but their commander was from the French-Spanish border. When he found out that Iñigo was from the same area, though across the border, he gave him some food and let him go. Iñigo was lucky again when he reached Genoa, a Spanish ally. One of the Spanish officers, who was in charge of protecting supply ships, turned out to be an old friend from their days together as **courtiers** at Arévalo. He took care of Iñigo's needs and got him a berth on a ship to Barcelona. The ship barely escaped the pursuit of French vessels under the famous admiral Andrea Doria. Having left Barcelona in mid-March 1523, Iñigo returned after almost precisely a year.

IV

Student Years in Barcelona, Alcalá, and Salamanca, 1524–1528

Iñigo's romantic dream of converting Muslims in Jerusalem had collapsed, at least for the time being. Now what was he to do with his life? He wanted to win people to Christ and reform their lives. Gradually he realized that to do so he would need a formal education very different from the training in courtly behavior he had had in his youth. Those manners would continue to serve him well to the day he died; he was more a people person than a scholar. He had a knack for winning people's confidence. He was already a master beggar, as has been and will be seen many times. Most people instinctively trusted him and were willing to help him because they saw in him transparent sincerity and high religious idealism. But not everyone. Again and again he would be denounced to the Inquisition and investigated, but each time he emerged vindicated. Many historians and at least one biographer have even seen him as a master Machiavellian, using his ability to win people over as a means of manipulating them.

Initially Iñigo intended to learn the rudiments of Latin grammar from a monk at Manresa who had befriended him the previous year. He went to Manresa, only to find that the monk had died. He then returned to the bustling port of Barcelona, where his two friends, Inés Pascal and Isabel Roser, opened their doors, purses, and hearts to him. Pascal provided him with a tiny attic room, only five feet high, where he could sleep and study. He refused her offer of a bed and slept on the floor. His friends also introduced him to Jerónimo Ardèvol, a skilled teacher who ran a grammar school. Ardèvol accepted him as a student without charging him tuition. Iñigo must have been a most unusual student, sitting in class behind boys in their early teens. He was now thirty-four and had seen more than most people did in a lifetime.

Latin was the key to higher education in every country from Poland to England for at that time all university classes were conducted in Latin. More books were being published in Latin than in all the vernacular languages combined, to say nothing of the vast majority of scholarly works. So Iñigo tried to master Latin declensions and conjugations, but with little success—every time he tried to concentrate, he was filled with spiritual insights far more vivid than those he experienced during the hours he gave to formal prayer. Eventually he decided that these moments of rapture were coming from the devil and not from God, because they were distracting him from his main task—getting the education that would enable him to work more effectively for God's glory. In *The Spiritual Exercises* Iñigo devoted two sections to what he called "Rules for the Discernment of Spirits"—how to tell whether movements of the heart and emotions come from God or not. In a meeting with Ardèvol he promised him his total attention for the two years he planned to study in Barcelona. The pledge worked, for his distractions ceased.

Ardèvol used the newly published humanist textbook by Antonio Nebrija, *Introduction to Latin Grammar,* which would have introduced him to the *Aeneid* of Virgil and selected proverbs drawn from the writings of the Stoic moralist Seneca. At the end of the two years, Ardèvol told him that he was ready to tackle university courses and recommended the University of Alcalá, then famous for integrating the new ideas of the Renaissance into its curriculum.

During his studies at Barcelona Iñigo continued to help people spiritually and to raise alms to help the many poor who crowded the city. Crucial to this work were his contacts with Isabel Roser, who belonged to the local nobility and introduced Iñigo to other noblewomen. One was Doña Estefanía Requeséns, whose husband was tutor to Prince Philip (later King Philip II). Another was Isabel de Josá, who, like Isabel Roser, later tried to become a woman Jesuit. Through his contacts with these wealthy women, Iñigo was able to secure funds to help the beggars who used to come to the gate of Inés Pascal's, house where Iñigo would distribute food. He also made the rounds and secretly gave food and alms to members of the lower nobility who had fallen on hard times; their noble status made begging and taking many jobs socially unacceptable for them. These "shamefaced poor" were found throughout sixteenth-century Europe but were especially numerous in Spain because it was hard hit by an inflation that undermined the income of the nobility and because Spain had a higher proportion of noblemen.

Iñigo also had contacts with nuns in three Barcelona convents. The most important was with Teresa Rejadella. Later in life, Iñigo wrote several of his best letters of spiritual advice to Rejadella. She belonged to the convent of the Poor Clares, an order founded by Saint Francis of Assisi and Saint Clare two centuries earlier. The order had a very strict rule, but the convent at Barcelona was dominated by daughters of noble parents who had deposited them there to avoid having to raise the large dowry that finding a suitable noble husband entailed. These noble nuns developed an easygoing lifestyle far from the austerity required by the rule of the Poor Clares, so in 1518 they arranged for the convent to switch to the less demanding Rule of Saint Benedict. Teresa Rejadella was the leader of a group of eleven nuns who wanted to restore the full observance of their old rule. Iñigo encouraged their efforts, and it almost cost him his life. Some of the nuns had lovers among the younger nobility. Had Rejadella and Iñigo succeeded in bringing back the strict rule of cloister, these young noblemen would have lost all contact with their friends. They jumped Iñigo and gave him a severe beating that kept him bedridden for two months.

While in Barcelona Iñigo gathered around him three young male disciples who accompanied him when he moved to the **University of Alcalá** and then to the **University of Salamanca.** Also during these years Iñigo was free of the stomach pains that had begun at Manresa; they were to return during his last years in Rome and were probably the cause of his death.

In March 1526 Iñigo walked from Barcelona to the university town of Alcalá, in central Spain not many miles east of Madrid. The university was very large by the standards of the day. While studying there from early March 1526 till June of the next year, he took a basic course in logic, plus two more-advanced courses for which he was not well prepared. One involved the works of Albert the Great (c. 1200–1284) on natural science. The other was based on the *Sentences* of Peter Lombard (c. 1095–1160), which had been the standard text for theology courses since the thirteenth century. Alcalá was famous for pioneering the integration of Renaissance humanist writers in its courses, but Iñigo seems to have studied little of these writers. In Barcelona he had learned enough Latin to follow the lectures, but he brought little or no background to his courses and as a result made little progress. The university lacked a structured core curriculum and allowed students to take almost any courses they wished. Iñigo, like many ambitious students through the centuries, seems to have dived into courses beyond his capabilities.

This was an important reason for his failure to make much academic progress, but even more important was his involvement in extracurricular activities—not the modern kind but, as he admitted in his autobiography, busying "himself in giving the **Spiritual Exercises** and teaching catechism." He helped many students and other people he met to make great spiritual progress. Indeed, he attracted considerable crowds when he taught catechism lessons. One student he helped at Alcalá was Martín de Olabe, who later became a Jesuit and taught theology with great success in Rome. He also became friends with two priests. The Portuguese Manuel Miona became his confessor and later entered the Jesuit order. The Spaniard Diego de Equía too became an important Jesuit many years later. Both Diego and his brother Miguel helped supply Iñigo's material needs at Alcalá. Miguel, an important publisher, had just put out a Spanish translation of the *Handbook of the Christian Soldier* by Desiderius Erasmus (c. 1467–1536), the most influential Christian humanist. It proved a bestseller.

Iñigo read the *Handbook,* in which Erasmus sums up his vision of Christian living. In it there was little that either Protestants or Catholics could object to, but because of Erasmus's severe criticism of Catholic practices in many of his other writings, Iñigo later discouraged their use. While Iñigo was studying at Alcalá, these works enjoyed enormous popularity among Spanish intellectuals. But gradually the Inquisition began to move against his writings, even though Erasmus, after initial sympathy for some of Martin Luther's ideas, had attacked Luther on several key questions.

The Spanish Inquisition had been set up to deal with Jews and Muslims, but in the 1520s it was turning its attention to new targets. Certainly, the rapid spread of Luther's teachings resulted in a defensive mentality among Spanish churchmen, but the ideas of Luther and other early Protestants found less support in Spain than elsewhere in Europe. The main new target of the Inquisition was an indigenous group called the **Alumbrados,** or the Enlightened Ones. In 1525 the Spanish Inquisition condemned forty-eight theses that, rightly or wrongly, it attributed to the Alumbrados. During Iñigo's years at Alcalá there were two main centers of Alumbrados, at nearby Toledo and at Seville. Those at Toledo stressed they had become so God-like that they could not sin, some of them claiming special revelations from God. The Sevillian Alumbrados were more closely linked to popular superstitions. The Inquisitors moved vigorously against the Alumbrados. There were no executions, but posters were put up asking people to denounce suspects to the Inquisition, and many people were forced to recant their beliefs or go into exile.

Repeatedly the local Inquisitors or their delegates moved against Iñigo while he was at Alcalá. In a letter of 1545 to the king of Portugal, Loyola noted that he had been the subject of eight different investigations. The first came in November 1526, when some witnesses denounced him to the Inquisition. They were alarmed because Iñigo was teaching Christian doctrine or catechism without any formal education; moreover, he and the three disciples from Barcelona who had joined him at Alcalá (Juan de Arteaga, Lope de Cáceres, and Calixto de Sa), plus a young French recruit, Jean Reynalde, were going about Alcalá wearing long gowns of cheap gray cloth similar to the habits worn by members of religious orders. Often they went barefoot. It was said that they claimed to be following the lifestyle of Christ's apostles, so it is hardly surprising that some people mistook Iñigo and his followers for Alumbrados. Iñigo had been living at the Hospital de la Misericordia. The Inquisitors questioned the manager of the hospital and his wife, but the charges were not very serious, and the Inquisitors turned the case over to a representative of the archbishop of Toledo, Juan Rodriguez de Figueroa, who questioned Iñigo and his companions. He found nothing blameworthy in what they were teaching, but he insisted that they should wear gowns of different colors—that way they could not be confused with members of a religious order.

In March of the next year, more serious charges arose since Iñigo had been teaching catechism and methods of prayer that he called Spiritual Exercises to small groups of people, mostly women, some of whom were converted prostitutes. Back in Barcelona, most of the women to whom Iñigo gave spiritual advice were from the upper classes; at Alcalá they were from the common people. Several depositions from the subsequent hearing have survived. The Spiritual Exercises were probably the methods of meditation or mental prayer that years later Loyola would spell out in his printed *The Spiritual Exercises*. Iñigo was also encouraging devout men and women to go to confession and receive communion weekly—something very rare in the late medieval church but a practice that others were already urging in Italy. After more than a month of questioning people and gathering notes, the authorities put Iñigo in prison for seventeen days. Again it was Archbishop Figueroa who asked him to explain what he had been doing and teaching. What seems to have precipitated his arrest was the disappearance of two of his followers, a mother and her daughter. Iñigo explained that they had wanted to go on pilgrimage to two distant shrines, one in southern Spain, the other near the Portuguese border. Although he had discouraged their plan because he knew the dangers they might run into, they had gone ahead. By May the women had returned and corroborated what he said. Figueroa passed sentence on June 1 and required Iñigo to abandon his eccentric dress and put on ordinary clothing. Since Loyola had no money for new clothes, Figueroa himself paid for them, so impressed was he by Iñigo. But he also warned Iñigo not to hold any more meetings until he had completed four more years of study. This Iñigo could not accept, for he was certain God was calling him to help souls. He therefore decided to leave Alcalá and carry on both his work and his education at Spain's other prestigious university, Salamanca.

One of the local women whom Figueroa called in to testify was Maria de la Flor, who had been a prostitute. She told how Iñigo had converted her and directed her through a partial version of the Spiritual Exercises. This is the first known case of what became a crucial tool for Iñigo and the later Jesuits in helping people to commit to God-centered living.

Iñigo reached Salamanca in early July 1527 and linked up with his four followers, who had arrived earlier. His stay there was something of a rerun of Alcalá, but worse. He picked a Dominican friar as his confessor, who some ten days later told him that the friars would like him and his follower Calixto de Sa to come to their convent for dinner and conversation. Most of the Inquisitors in Spain were Dominicans, who saw themselves as the guardians of Catholic orthodoxy. After supper, the confessor together with two other friars brought Iñigo and Calixto to their chapel and began questioning them. Loyola's autobiography summarizes their conversation. The friars conceded that they had heard good reports about his morals and piety, but they were worried about his trying to teach the common folk about religion. What training did he and his companions have? He told them that he and his followers did not have much education in theology, but they did not preach and held only spiritual conversations on topics such as the virtues and vices. One friar implied that, if they were uneducated, they must be claiming to speak through the Holy Spirit. This put Iñigo on his guard, and he tried to break off the conversation, but one friar went on to imply that he was spreading the errors of Erasmus. Iñigo now refused to speak unless under obligation. He and Calixto remained shut up in the convent for three days while some of the friars tried to launch an official investigation. Meanwhile Iñigo conversed with other friars, mainly in the dining hall. Some took his side.

Then an official came to the convent, took Iñigo and Calixto to the local prison and had them chained up. As word of this spread through the town, friends came to bring the two prisoners clothes and necessities and listen to their explanations of Christian doctrine. When an official asked for a copy of the Spiritual Exercises, Iñigo gave him his notes to examine. Two more of his other followers were brought in and locked in the same cell. The hearing was held before four judges who had examined the Exercises. They questioned him closely on the text and on theological questions—for instance, on the Trinity, the sacraments, and the Ten Commandments—and were satisfied by his answers. Then they brought up the delicate distinction between mortal and venial sins. They found nothing to condemn in his explanation, but they believed that men untrained in theology should not be teaching others about this question. Several important men visited him in prison, including the cardinal-archbishop of Burgos, who asked him how he was bearing up in prison. Iñigo replied that Salamanca did not have as many chains as he wanted to bear for the love of God.

A few days later there was a massive jail break. Only Iñigo and his companions did not take the opportunity to escape. That impressed people. After Iñigo and Calixto had spent twenty-two days in prison, the judges passed sentence. It was milder than the sentence at Alcalá: the judges found nothing wrong with the morals or teaching of Iñigo and his companions, so they were free to keep teaching, but they should avoid speaking about differences between mortal and venial sins until they had four more years of study. Iñigo said that he would obey the sentence as long as he stayed at Salamanca, but he objected that it hindered his ability to help souls. He therefore decided to leave Spain and go to Paris, where he could study at the most famous university in the world. A new chapter in his life was opening.

What happened to Iñigo's four companions from his days at Alcalá and Salamanca? He planned for them to follow him to Paris and kept contact with them by letters, but gradually they drifted away. Their brief contact with him seems to have had lasting effect on the lives of two of them. Jean Reynalde became a Franciscan friar. Juan de Arteaga served briefly as bishop of Chiapas in Mexico, where he became ill. The people ministering to him accidently gave him poison to drink and killed him. Calixto de Sa also went to Mexico, where he became a merchant and returned to Salamanca with considerable wealth. Lope de Cáceres went back to his native Segovia and seems to have abandoned much interest in religion.

The University of Paris, 1528–1535

When Iñigo left Salamanca, he was undecided about what he would do with the rest of his life. He seriously considered entering a religious order. He leaned toward an unreformed order because he could work toward its reform. Undoubtedly such work would face opposition from older monks who did not want to lose an easy lifestyle, but he considered this an advantage because their opposition would afford him an opportunity to suffer for Christ's sake. As he said in his autobiography, "God made him very confident that he could bear up well under all the insults and indignities that might be inflicted on him." But he rejected this option and decided to go to Paris and continue his studies.

Although he was undoubtedly attracted by the excellent reputation that the University of Paris enjoyed, he also felt that studying in a foreign country where he could not speak the language would prevent him from lavishing too much time and energy on helping the townspeople at the expense of his studies. There would still be many Spanish students in Paris whom he could win to holy living. Up to this point the audience for his spiritual advice had been mainly women. In Paris it would of necessity be men, for universities of that day were open to men only and, since Loyola could not speak French, his dealings with women would be very restricted.

If he were to study in Paris, he would need money. When he went to Jerusalem, he had refused to take any money with him, trusting that God would provide. Now he obviously regarded this as devout but impractical. Significantly, when he left Salamanca in mid-September, he had a donkey loaded with his books. He spent about three months in Barcelona, visiting his benefactors, including Isabel Roser and Inés Pascual, and gathering alms. He had not expected to spend so much time there, but war had broken out again between Charles V and Francis I, and stories were circulating around Barcelona about how the French were roasting Spaniards alive on spits, so his friends tried to discourage his going. He persisted and, walking on foot, he arrived in Paris on 2 February 1528.

Although he was now thirty-seven, Ignatius decided that he would start over and join teenagers in taking the basic curriculum. It was a wise choice. He not only gained the background he needed to do well in advanced courses but also came to know and appreciate the planned curriculum at Paris, known as the *modus Parisiensis.* This Paris mode of courses building one on another in an ordered sequence became the cornerstone of the Jesuit **Ratio Studiorum,** or Plan of Studies, whose foundation Loyola laid in the Jesuit Constitutions. A final version of the Ratio, enriched by fifty years' experience, was issued in 1599 and laid down regulations for Jesuit colleges that remained in effect for three centuries.

In Paris Iñigo may have changed his name to Ignatius, or it may have been changed inadvertently by a university official in registering him, and he kept the change for the rest of his life. *Iñigo* was a Spanish name that would have been unfamiliar to most Frenchmen. Saint Ignatius of Antioch was a famous bishop and writer, who was martyred at Rome about A.D. 107.

Initially Ignatius lived and studied at the College of Montaigu, which offered some courses but was also a residential college similar to a modern university dormitory. The rules were old-fashioned and very strict. Two great writers had lived there before Ignatius, Erasmus and François Rabelais (1494–1553). They hated the experience and mocked the college in their writings, Erasmus associating the college with rotten eggs and ravenous lice, Rabelais claiming that students came out either fools or lifetime invalids. Ignatius was made of tougher stuff, but soon he too left the college, though not because of its regulations.

At the college were several Spanish students with whom he became friendly. For safekeeping he entrusted to one of them the bill of exchange on a merchant's account for all the money he had raised in Barcelona. His friend cashed it and went on a binge. Ignatius was now a penniless beggar who could not afford to live at the college. He found lodgings at a hospice for pilgrims traveling to the shrine of St. James at Compostella in northern Spain, but the hospice was on the right bank of the Seine River; the university was on the left bank in the Latin Quarter (so called because so many students were speaking Latin there). The distance between the college and the hospice required thirty minutes of brisk walking. Worse, the hospice did not open its doors before sunrise, while classes at the college started at five A.M. In the evening things were no better: the hospice closed its doors at sunset, so that Ignatius could not attend evening functions at the university.

Ignatius thought he had an answer to his problem: professors often employed students as servants. A couple of respected men at the university wrote letters of recommendation for him, but no professor was willing to employ him. The job would have provided Ignatius with either free lodging or enough money to rent a room close to the college. Fortunately a Spanish friar suggested an alternative. There were many wealthy Spanish merchants in the main Belgian trading cities of Bruges and Antwerp. Why not go there and ask for their support? As always, Ignatius proved to be the master beggar. He went to Belgium in 1529, 1530, and 1531. In 1531 he also went across the English Channel to visit London and raised even more money than before—so much that he was able to help other poor students.

Juan Polanco, who was Loyola's secretary toward the end of his life, tells an interesting story about a dinner Ignatius attended during his 1529 visit to Bruges. The host was the most famous of all the Spanish humanists, Juan Luis Vives (1492–1540). It was Lent, and conversation turned to the Lenten fast imposed on all Catholics. Vives noted ironically that this was a pseudopenance since there were all sorts of tasty sea foods available. Ignatius countered: "You and others who can dine elegantly may not find much help from this abstinence for the purpose the church intends, but most people, whose welfare the church must keep in mind, cannot dine so elegantly and so have an opportunity for mortifying their bodies and doing penance." It seems that Vives, far from taking offense, was impressed by the middle-aged student.

On returning to Paris in September of 1529 Ignatius received a letter from the student who had cashed in his letter of credit and squandered his money: the student lay ill and destitute at Rouen in Normandy. Could Ignatius help him? He decided to walk the whole distance barefoot and fasting. His resolution filled him with fear of endangering his health, but he set off and after nine miles was filled with such spiritual joy that he shouted aloud his thanks to the Lord. The trip took three days. At Rouen he helped his friend until he was able to sail back to Spain. Ignatius gave him funds to cover his travel expenses and asked him to carry back some letters.

When Ignatius returned to Paris, he found himself under a cloud of hostility. Previously he had given the Spiritual Exercises to three Spaniards, two of whom were already teaching at the university. This seems the first time that he directed anyone through the complete thirty days of the Exercises. Of the three students, one later became a Carthusian monk, and the second returned to Spain and became a famous preacher in Toledo. The third, Amador de Elduayen, involved Ignatius in immediate trouble with Diogo de Gouveia, the headmaster of the College of Saint Barbe, to which Ignatius had recently transferred. Gouveia believed that Ignatius had turned Elduayen into a fool. Indeed, all of the three lost interest in academic pursuits, so Gouveia threatened Ignatius with a public penance called the Sala or the Hall: the faculty and students would gather in the main hall of the college, where Ignatius would be stripped to the waist and whipped. When he heard of these plans, Ignatius went to the Inquisitor of Paris and asked that the punishment be administered on the first day of class so he could get on with his studies without this affair hanging over his head. The Inquisitor noted that he had heard complaints but said he planned to do nothing.

The storm subsided gradually, then arose again. Ignatius and the three students began holding Sunday discussions and prayer meetings that included mass, confession, and communion at a nearby Carthusian monastery. Unfortunately these meetings overlapped the time for the college's public disputations, and gradually the number of students going to his meetings grew while the group going to the disputations declined. He was warned about this but did nothing, so Gouveia once more scheduled a Sala. Ignatius was not worried about the pain and shame involved in the punishment, but he was concerned it might alienate some students. He therefore went to Gouveia and explained what he and his friends were doing and why. The Sala was held, but before the punishment began, Gouveia, who was a deeply religious man, knelt before Ignatius and asked for his pardon, much to the astonishment of the students and faculty. Thereafter the headmaster and Ignatius were on the best of terms. Gouveia even changed the time for the disputations so it would not conflict with Loyola's Sunday gatherings.

Diogo de Gouveia, headmaster at Paris, asks for forgiveness.

In contrast to Alcalá and Salamanca, Ignatius cut back his work for souls in Paris so that he could devote more time and energy to his studies. Unfortunately, the experience he had in Barcelona started to return: whenever he tried to concentrate on philosophy, he was engulfed in spiritual consolation. Again he attributed this to the devil; again he went to his professor, Juan Peña, and promised to attend every lecture and give his full concentration. Once again the temptations to rapturous daydreaming stopped.

The bachelor of arts program took Ignatius three years. Its emphasis was philosophy, as had been traditional in medieval universities. During the second year students spent much of their time in disputations and study of Aristotle's writings on logic. The disputations sharpened students' skill in constructing their own logical arguments and refuting weak arguments. Students then advanced to Aristotle's works on physics, metaphysics, and ethics. While Latin translations of Aristotle were the main textbooks, students were sometimes expected to consult the Greek original. Here Ignatius was weak, but fortunately he could consult his learned roommate Peter Faber (Pierre Favre), a Savoyard, who quickly became his closest disciple in Paris. Faber helped Loyola with Greek; Loyola helped Faber overcome his religious scruples.

At the end of their third year students had to pass a final examination of great severity, one part in public, the other in private before four professors. Ignatius ranked thirtieth out of one hundred students. Ignatius was never a great scholar, but his ranking was excellent for a man of forty. Those who passed the examination were granted the licentiate degree on 13 March 1533. The licentiate gave students the legal right to teach anywhere in the world, but finding a job was another matter. The master of arts degree required no new courses or examinations but did require heavy expenses and was celebrated with great pomp, including a lecture by the candidate. Students receiving the degree were then enrolled on the list of Paris professors. Ignatius had to postpone taking the degree until he could raise the money. Meanwhile he devoted himself to studying theology. His master's diploma still exists and is dated (by our calendar) 14 March 1535. Henceforward, he was addressed as Master Ignatius.

Loyola's studies at Paris were to have long-lasting effects. As has been seen, Aristotle's works dominated the undergraduate curriculum during his Paris years, as they had in the thirteenth century. The study of Aristotle's philosophy retained a large role in the Jesuit colleges that began to spread across Europe in the 1550s. In the later Middle Ages the writings of Saint Thomas Aquinas (c. 1225–1274) were often overshadowed by later theologians such as John Duns Scotus (c. 1266–1308) and William of Ockham (c. 1285–1347), but Thomism (the theology of Aquinas) made a comeback in the early sixteenth century. In Italy the revival of Thomism was led by Thomas de Vio, known as Cajetan (1469–1534), who was later general of the Dominican Order and an influential cardinal. In Salamanca Francisco de Vitoria (1492–1546) sparked the revival. In Paris the leader of the Thomistic revival was the Scotsman John Mair, who taught at the College of Saint Barbe while Ignatius was a student there; another distinguished professor was Mair's gifted disciple the Belgian Pierre Crockaert. Years later, when Loyola wrote the rules governing the colleges of the Jesuit Order, he made Aquinas the Jesuits' preferred theologian. Aquinas, supported by both the Dominicans and Jesuits, was to exert an influence second to none on Roman Catholic theology from the sixteenth century until the 1960s and beginning of the Second Vatican Council. Loyola's own optimistic view of the created world as reflecting God's grandeur, expressed most clearly in the last meditation of his Spiritual Exercises, mirrors the teaching of Aquinas.

Had Loyola died while in Paris, he would have been utterly unknown to historians, merely a name on a list of students in the university archives. But in Paris he recruited a group of companions whom he inspired with his religious ideals. Together, after some false starts, they founded the **Society of Jesus,** known as the Jesuits. At Saint Barbe he was assigned to share a room with two other young men. Never has the assignment of roommates at a college had greater long-range consequences. His roommates were Peter Faber (1506–1546) and **Francis Xavier** (1506–1552). We have already noted how Faber helped Ignatius with the Greek text of Aristotle. He was born in the village of Villaret in Savoy. Savoy was ruled by an Italian duke whose domains spread on both the French and Italian sides of the Alps. Peter was from the French part. As a young lad he worked as a shepherd but had an intense desire for an education. At Paris he proved a brilliant student in both philosophy and theology, but he was besieged by scruples and guilt feelings. He considered becoming a priest but could not make up his mind. Ignatius had himself fought and won battles with religious scruples and so was able to help his roommate conquer them. They became fast friends, the younger man looking to Ignatius for guidance. In the fall of 1533 Faber returned to his home village, visited his family, and settled his affairs. Returning to Paris, he spent a month during the coldest part of an unusually severe winter following the Spiritual Exercises in a Paris suburb. Ignatius was his guide or director, visiting several times a week to confer with him and propose meditations drawn from the Spiritual Exercises. So enthusiastic was Faber that he imposed a very severe fast on himself and refused to heat his room. When Ignatius found this out, he forbade Peter to continue his penances since, though undoubtedly springing from religious zeal, they were likely to undermine his health and thereby permanently harm his ability to serve God. During his retreat Faber decided to become a priest so that he could minister to others. He was ordained 30 May 1534.

Francis Xavier, like Ignatius, was a nobleman from the Basque country of northern Spain. In the same French invasion during which Loyola was wounded at Pamplona, Xavier's relatives fought on the side of the French. After the French defeat, the castle of Xavier's family was stripped of its fortifications. Xavier could have little hope for a career in Spain. Largely barred from a career in Spain, Xavier went instead to Paris, where he was successful as a student and planned to make an academic career in France. He became well-known around the university as a fine athlete. While he was the roommate of Loyola and Faber, he was teaching philosophy at the College of Saint Beauvais, one of the university's many colleges. Loyola attended some of his classes and encouraged other students to do the same. Xavier rebuffed Loyola's first efforts to entice him to devote his life to God's service. Xavier could expect little money from his family and had run up a debt in earning his degree. Loyola helped him financially, but in their conversations he kept asking Xavier hard questions about life's meaning and gradually won him over. Indeed, Loyola and Faber had to persuade Xavier not to quit his teaching position in mid semester. Because Xavier had signed a commitment to teach for three and a half years, he was unable to devote a full month to carrying out the Spiritual Exercises until late in 1534. Later Xavier proved a brilliant missionary in India, Indonesia, and Japan.

Ignatius did not have to work so hard to win over two other young but gifted students. Diego Laínez (1511–1565) and Alfonso Salmerón (1515–1585) were friends who had studied at the University of Alcalá, where they heard many stories about a certain Iñigo. They decided to complete their education in Paris. Although only twenty, Laínez already had his master's degree when he set off. Salmerón was only seventeen. They decided to look up this Iñigo character when they reached Paris. Chance plays a larger role in history than most historians care to admit. As the two rode into Paris, they were confused about directions in the enormous city. The first person to greet them as they were about to unsaddle their mules was this Iñigo. He led them to good lodgings and had little trouble in making them his friends and sharing his ideals with them. Both were to become leading theologians at the Council of Trent. Laínez became the second superior general of the Jesuits after Loyola's death. Salmeron when on to publish exhaustive commentaries on the Bible.

Simon Rodrigues (1510–1579) was a Portuguese noble-man who joined Ignatius and his companions in 1533. He was supported at the College of Saint Barbe by a scholar-ship provided by the Portuguese king. He was handsome and had polished manners but was less intellectually gifted than the others and could be imprudent and moody. Later in life he would be a favorite of King John of Portugal and head of the fastest growing wing of the Jesuit order.

Nicolás Bobadilla (1507–1590) came from a peasant background in northern Spain. He had studied philosophy and theology at Alcalá and Valladolid before coming to Paris, where Ignatius helped him get a minor teaching post at one of the colleges. He was less interested in scholarship than were Loyola's other companions at Paris. Although he later proved a gifted preacher, Bobadilla could be out-spoken, impatient, pigheaded, and quarrelsome. As Salmerón commented, he was inclined to talk too much and interrupt others.

Gradually Loyola and his six companions grew closer together, wanting to be "friends in the Lord" and draw others to God. Several of them shared the same lodging and even a common purse. All the companions carried out the Spiritual Exercises under Loyola's direction except for Xavier, who made them under Faber. All but one of Loyola's companions took a month off to make the Exercises and took up lodging at a distance from their usual quarters so as to have maximum privacy. Loyola would visit them several times a week and lay out what they were to pray over for the coming day or days. They usually began with a fairly severe fast, but Loyola later dropped this.

Meanwhile Protestant ideas and converts were spreading to Paris and France. The very real shortcomings of Catholic churchmen and the criticism of Erasmus and other humanists had alienated many people from institutional Catholicism. The books of Martin Luther were being smuggled into France and sometimes openly sold in bookstores. Luther's teachings on justification by faith alone and on the Bible as the sole criterion for faith and religious practice seemed a liberating message to many Frenchmen, particularly among the nobility, merchants, and many craftsmen in most cities. Paris, however, remained a stronghold of Catholicism, and most of the theologians in Paris were conservative or even militant Catholics.

King Francis I found Erasmus more attractive than Luther, and he was reluctant to launch outright persecution. Several misguided actions of the Paris Protestants backfired, leading the king to act against them. In 1533 Nicholas Cop, a friend of John Calvin and a secret Protestant, was named rector of the university. In his inaugural address on 1 November 1533, Cop strongly advocated Luther's theology of justification and thereby stirred the Inquisition to action. Calvin and others had to flee Paris and even France. Far greater were the repercussions from the Affair of Placards, 17 October 1534. At dawn militant Protestants had posted placards in the public squares of Paris, Orléans, and other leading cities. One placard was even attached to the door of the king's bedchamber. Printed in Switzerland and smuggled into France, the placards bore in large print the title "The true articles against the horrible, gross and indefensible doctrine of the popish mass." Francis I encouraged the hunt for the perpetrators; six people were executed and dozens were thrown into prison. When in January the placards were posted again, the king led a procession of prayer and repentance in Paris, issued restrictions on the press, and executed six more Protestants. Direct evidence is lacking, but Loyola and his companions very likely watched the procession and applauded the executions, as did most of the people of Paris and the university faculty. Later the Jesuits were strongly opposed to Protestantism. They very rarely served as Inquisitors, not because they were opposed to the Inquisition on principle but because the Inquisition was dominated by friars, especially Dominicans.

Ignatius showed little interest in Protestantism while at Paris. His zeal turned elsewhere. His dream was to return to Jerusalem with his Paris companions and work for souls there, not to fight Protestantism in Europe. On 15 August 1534 Ignatius and his six companions climbed the hill of Montmartre, which overlooks Paris. There in a small chapel Faber, the only priest among them, celebrated mass. Just before communion each of them made a vow that he would devote his life to helping his neighbors while living a life of strict poverty but that he would do so only after they had made a pilgrimage to Jerusalem together. It is not clear if the vow to go to Jerusalem involved staying there and working to help pilgrims and perhaps convert Muslims to Christianity. If so, the goal was quite impractical: rarely have Muslims been inclined to convert to Christianity. Indeed, such converts faced capital punishment in Muslim countries, and the Turks who controlled Palestine would never have permitted Christian proselytism. The companions committed themselves to gather at Venice and seek a ship bound for Palestine. They also vowed to go to Rome and put themselves at the pope's disposal if, after a year of trying, they found it impossible to go to Jerusalem. Many historians have incorrectly dated the foundation of the Society of Jesus to these vows at Montmartre. The companions did not decide to found a religious order, and thereby to give their friendship a permanent form, until five years later.

Meanwhile Ignatius was continuing to study theology. He never received a degree, although the University of Paris gave him a certificate saying he had studied theology

Loyola and his six Paris companions vow to make a pilgrimage to Jerusalem.

there for a year and a half, and he later studied informally at Venice for more than a year. Two of the men who knew Loyola best, Jerónimo Nadal and Diego Laínez, commented on his theological learning. Nadal stressed his diligence, getting up before dawn and walking to the Dominican convent to attend lectures on Aquinas. Laínez also commended the same quality: despite being a poor linguist, he could hold his own in theological discussions with his companions, three of whom—Faber, Laínez and Salmerón—were gifted scholars.

Apparently as a result of his theological training and his encounters with Protestant teaching in Paris, Ignatius added an appendix to *The Spiritual Exercises* entitled "Rules for Thinking with the Church." In these rules he urges that those making the Spiritual Exercises put aside their own opinions and give an eager obedience to the hierarchical church. They should defend going to mass and confession and receiving communion, clerical celibacy and religious orders, and traditional devotion to relics, fasting, and church art. In agreement with Erasmus he encourages respect for bishops and writers of the early church (the Church Fathers) but, contrary to Erasmus and many humanists, he also praises medieval scholastics such as Aquinas. Christians should be careful when they talk about predestination, lest the common folk conclude that they need no longer worry about virtuous living. Their conversations should stress the need for both faith and good works and not so exalt the power of grace that it seems to deny free will.

Some scholars have argued that still other passages in the *Exercises* were influenced by Ignatius's Paris training. In March 1535 hostile rumors about Ignatius and the Exercises, were circulating through the city. Ignatius was planning to leave Paris and return to Spain, but he wanted to put a stop to these rumors once and for all. He therefore gave a handwritten copy of the *Exercises* to the

Paris Inquisitor, the Dominican friar Valentin Liévin, and asked him to approve or disapprove them. Ignatius wanted Liévin to give a formal sentence, but Liévin hesitated. Finally Ignatius brought in a notary who wrote down his discussions with Liévin. Thus Loyola secured a formal approval of the Exercises. On later occasions when his orthodoxy was challenged, Loyola pursued a similar strategy. Scholars today would love to examine the copy given Liévin and the earlier one that he gave the Inquisitors at Salamanca, for they would reveal how the *Exercises* evolved from Loyola's notebook at Manresa down through his Paris studies. Alas, no such copies exist. Chapter 9 will examine the development and content of the Spiritual Exercises.

VI

Loyola Returns to Spain, 1535

Ignatius had three reasons for returning to Spain in early May 1535. The most pressing was his health. Through much of his life he endured stomach pains, which seem to have resulted from gall stones. Now that the problem was getting worse, Ignatius consulted doctors at Paris, but when their suggested remedies did no good, they resorted to a prescription much employed by bewildered doctors in that era: "The patient must return to his native air." Presumably it was the air or water or something about Paris that was causing the trouble; if Ignatius could return home, where he had enjoyed a healthy childhood, the doctors believed, his native air would restore his health.

Ignatius had two other reasons for returning. He needed to visit the families of several of his six companions to settle their affairs, for they would be going off to Jerusalem, maybe never to return. Finally, Ignatius was painfully aware that in his youth he had not set a good example of Christian living. He wanted to return home so that the people who had known the old Iñigo might see the new Ignatius whom God had changed.

When Ignatius mounted a horse that his companions had bought for him and headed south toward northern Spain and his hometown of Azpeitia in the Basque country, he had been gone for thirteen years. According to their plans, he and his Paris companions, after completing their studies, would gather at Venice on 25 January 1537 to make arrangements for their voyage to Palestine. Ignatius was determined that he would not stay with his brother Martín García in Castle Loyola, but would find lodging at Azpeitia in the Magdalena Hospice (the local refuge for the homeless), from which he could work to help the townsfolk in body and soul. Since he wanted to avoid Castle Loyola, he decided that he would travel incognito and not send advance notice of his coming to his family or friends there.

On the journey several things happened. The best was that his health was already improving as he rode south. When he stopped in the French city of Bayonne, someone recognized him and sent word to his brother Martín García, who then sent two men to meet and help Ignatius on his journey. Loyola's autobiography relates the sequel. As he crossed the border into his native province of **Guipúzcoa,** he deliberately avoided the main road and took a minor path—one that was famous for lurking brigands. He spotted two armed men coming toward him, but they passed him by. Suddenly they turned and hurried back toward him. Ignatius admits that he was struck by fear, but he managed to engage his pursuers in a conversation. It turned out that they were the two servants that his brother Martín García had sent in search of him. Ignatius persuaded them to ride ahead while he continued at a slower pace. He then took a route that skirted Loyola Castle and headed toward Azpeitia and the Magdalena Hospice. The two men caught up with him again and tried to persuade him to come to the castle, but he refused.

Considerable documentation survives about Ignatius work at Azpeitia, where he stayed from late April to late

July 1535. When investigators were gathering evidence for his canonization in 1595, they visited Azpeitia; nineteen people came forward and testified that they had seen and heard him sixty years earlier. Clearly he made a lasting impression. He refused to visit the family castle despite repeated pleas from his family. He continued to beg his bread from door to door, no doubt to the horror of his brother Martín García. Every day he gathered a group of children and taught them catechism. Even Martín García came to listen. Sometimes he preached out of doors to adults, but his brother Pero, the local pastor, also allowed him to preach in the town church on Sundays, even though he had not been ordained. One of his sermons, which made a deep impression and was remembered long after, was preached at a local shrine where crowds from several towns had flocked. So he could be better seen and heard, Ignatius climbed a plum tree. The man whose gallant youth and romances were still remembered then launched into a denunciation of vices, dwelling on a practice of the local concubines. The local custom was for unmarried girls to go bareheaded; married women wore bonnets. But then concubines started wearing bonnets so they could pass for married women. Many of them wept during his sermon. Urged by Ignatius, local magistrates introduced legislation forbidding concubines to wear bonnets.

Often his preaching dwelt on the Ten Commandments. He attacked gambling and induced three prostitutes to reform their lives, including one noted for her beauty, Magdalena de Mendiola. Years later she went on a pilgrimage to Jerusalem and Rome, where she visited Ignatius. As his reputation grew, he was able to work out a compromise solution to a long-standing controversy between the local clergy and a convent of Franciscan nuns.

One day he agreed to go to Loyola Castle and spend the night, complying with the request of his sister-in-law. One of his relatives (probably Martín García, her husband) used to have a concubine sneak into the castle by a secret door. As the concubine was entering, Ignatius confronted her, had a long talk with her, and kept her from going to her lover.

While at Azpeitia he introduced a custom that was becoming widespread: in the town church and in nearby villages the church bells would be rung at noon as a signal to the people to kneel and recite two prayers for those who had fallen into serious sin and two more that they themselves might never fall that way. When Martín García made out his will years later, he set up permanent funding to pay bell ringers for this service.

Ignatius's most important contribution to his hometown was in reforming how it dealt with poor people. New legislation was introduced that forbade begging,

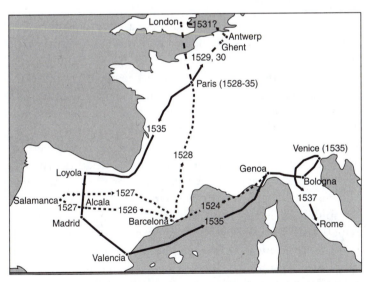

After completing secondary studies in Barcelona, Loyola attended the universities of Alcalá, Salamanca, and Paris. In 1529–1531 he made fund-raising trips to Belgium and England. After returning to Spain in 1535, he went to Venice for two years, then settled in Rome in 1537 for the rest of his life.

but two town officials were to collect donations and then give alms to poor people whose names were recorded on an official list. Help was also given to poor people who were too ashamed to beg. Able-bodied men were expected to work for a living. This was the approach advocated by Juan Luis Vives in his 1526 book *On Helping the Poor;* many towns throughout Europe were adopting similar legislation, a fact that Ignatius probably knew. At Azpeitia his shabby dark brown cloak and hemp sandals undoubtedly were embarrassing to his family. As he prepared to leave, some of them came and persuaded him to accept a horse and some money and allow Martín García and others to accompany him to the border of Navarre. When they turned back, he got rid of the horse, distributed his money to the poor, and walked to Pamplona.

Before going on to Italy and Venice Ignatius still had to contact the relatives of his companions and try to settle their affairs. This task took him to Almazán, Sigüenza, Madrid, Toledo, and Valencia and lasted four months. When he visited the Xavier family, he found that both Xavier's parents and two of his sisters had died recently. Two of Xavier's brothers, who had helped the French invasion in which Loyola was wounded, had received an amnesty from Emperor Charles V, had settled down, and had married. Ignatius gave Xavier's brother Juan, who had married a rich widow and was living at Obanos, near Pamplona, a letter from Francis. Included in the letter, which still survives, was warm praise for Ignatius that helped offset his scruffy appearance and the hostile rumors about him that Juan seems to have heard. Xavier asked Juan to send him some funds, for he was living "in great poverty." Ignatius would bring him the money.

At Almazán he delivered a letter from Diego Laínez to his father, a wealthy businessman, who then transferred funds to his son in Paris. It seems that at Madrid he met the young prince, later Philip II, Spain's most famous king. Ignatius must have made a strong impression on the eight-year-old, for when in 1586 he saw the portrait of Loyola by Alonso Sánchez Coelho, Philip recalled their meeting and commented, "I met Father Ignatius and this is certainly his face, but he had more beard when I saw him." Toledo lies just south of Madrid, and there Ignatius met with the family of Alfonso Salmerón. During these journeys he also looked up his old disciples from Alcalá, but they had settled down and could not be won over to the Palestine project.

This part of his mission accomplished, Ignatius headed for the port of Valencia, where he caught a ship to Genoa and Italy, probably in November. The trip was eventful. A Turkish fleet under the famous pirate-admiral Khaireddin, known as Barbarossa, was said to be operating nearby. Reports, erroneous as it turned out, claimed that the Turks had already killed a thousand Christians on Minorca and taken 4,000 prisoners while other Turkish ships were ravaging the Sardinian coast. These reports did not discourage Loyola from sailing, but his ship ran into something worse than a Turkish fleet. A severe storm cost the ship its anchor, and most of the people on board expected to die, but the ship was able to limp into Genoa.

VII

From Venice to Rome, 1536–1540

Winter was just beginning when Ignatius arrived in Genoa. He planned to walk the 180 miles to Bologna, where he hoped to continue his study of theology. The University of Bologna, founded in 1088, was the oldest university in the world and still enjoyed considerable prestige. Not only was the weather cold and wet, but Ignatius had to cross the Apennines, the mountain range that forms the north-south spine of Italy. As he was climbing a small ridge above a river gorge, he lost his way, and his path became increasingly narrow and steep. Soon he found himself crawling on his knees, trapped so that he could not even turn and go back lest he slip into the gorge. In his autobiography he called this the most exhausting physical experience of his life. To make matters worse, as he entered Bologna on a narrow footbridge, he slipped and fell into a river. As he climbed out covered with mud, the onlookers broke into laughter and rained nasty comments on his head: not a good beginning for the first day at a new university. For a whole week he traversed the city begging alms. Normally he was the master beggar, but the

Bolognese would not give him anything. He did not formally enroll in the College of San Clement, but the college had many Spanish students, and Ignatius seems to have lodged with them in a boardinghouse. Toward the end of February his stomach pains grew so intense that for seven straight days he was confined to bed with alternating chills and fever. After he recovered, he decided that the climate at Bologna was bad for his health, so he moved to Venice, where his companions and he were scheduled to rendezvous toward the end of the year. The climate was milder there, but since Venice had no university, he had to study theology on his own.

Just as during his earlier stay at Venice while awaiting a ship to Jerusalem, Ignatius was able to find influential benefactors. He seems to have stayed at the home of Andrea Lippomano, a member of a prominent noble family and the prior of the Monastery of the Most Holy Trinity. Later Lippomano provided major funding for Jesuit schools in Venice and Padua. The previous year Lippomano had hosted Saint Girolamo Emiliani (1481–1537), a tough former soldier who in 1528 founded a small religious order in Venice known as the Somaschi. Its members devoted themselves to helping the poor and marginalized, especially plague victims. Emiliani died from plague he contracted while caring for the sick. It is uncertain whether the two saints ever met, but Loyola certainly would have heard about Emiliani and his followers from Lippomano and others. In Venice Loyola's health improved, and money sent by Isabel Roser, his longtime benefactor in Barcelona, provided for his material needs. Studying theology did not take all of his time—he gave the Spiritual Exercises to at least four men whom he mentions. One was Pietro Contarini, a member of a famous Venetian family who later became a bishop. Another was the Spaniard Diego de Hoces, who had just returned from a pilgrimage to Jerusalem. Hoces was attracted to making the Exercises, but (he told Ignatius) he had also heard that they contained evil doctrine, so he had brought along some books to refute any heresy. He found no heresy, and shortly after making the Exercises Hoces became one of Loyola's closeknit companions.

The reluctance of Hoces to making the Exercises has often been traced to his previous contacts with Gianpietro Carafa (1479–1559), the bishop of Chieti. During Loyola's last twenty years, Carafa was his most dangerous opponent. He was named a cardinal in December 1537 and became Pope Paul IV in 1555. Rumors were swirling around Venice that Ignatius had been condemned repeatedly by the Spanish Inquisition and had been burned in effigy in Spain and Paris. Carafa probably did not invent these slanders, but he seems to have passed them on to Hoces. Apparently he was bitterly disappointed when Hoces did not enter the Theatines, a new religious order that Carafa had helped to found in 1524. He was deeply religious but impetuous and utterly intransigent in his views.

Sometime in 1536 Loyola wrote a letter to Carafa in which he criticized several practices of the Theatine Order. It seems the letter was never sent, but Carafa somehow came to know its contents. The letter is important because it makes clear that three years before the foundation of the Jesuits Loyola was already thinking about how a new religious order should be structured to face the pastoral needs of the church in the Reformation era. In his letter he criticized the Theatines for forbidding the begging of alms, instead simply awaiting the spontaneous generosity of benefactors. Most of the Theatines lived an austere lifestyle, but Carafa himself, a rich nobleman and bishop, did not. Ignatius urged that he should follow the example of Saint Francis and Saint Dominic, the founders of the Franciscans and Dominicans, in cultivating simplicity. Ignatius also believed that the Theatines should have devoted themselves more to preaching, hearing confessions, and performing works of mercy for poor and dying people. Undoubtedly the prickly Carafa saw the letter as impudent, the product of a scruffy Spanish layman suspected of heresy who dared to criticize an established scholar and bishop. Carafa was as eager for church reform as Loyola was, but right down to their deaths they differed radically on how this should be accomplished.

During the two years Loyola's companions had been completing their studies at Paris, they had added three new recruits: Claude Jay (1504–1562), Paschase Broët (1500–1562), and Jean Codure (1508–1541). Jay was from Savoy, some twenty miles from Faber's birthplace, while the other two were Frenchmen. The nine companions left Paris on 15 November 1536 and spent fifty-four days walking to Venice, partly because they could not take a direct route. War had again broken out between Francis I of France and Emperor Charles V. The French army invaded Savoy, whose duke was allied to Charles V. The emperor's army invaded southern France, only to be driven back. To avoid these contested areas Loyola's companions walked east from Paris to Strasbourg, then down the Rhine to Basel. Strasbourg was a Lutheran town but part of the empire, thus owing a vague allegiance to Charles V. Basel, in Switzerland, had accepted Zwingli's theology. Most of their other major stops were in Catholic cities—Constance, Bolzano, and Trent. The nine companions wore their long student gowns tucked up for easier walking; they carried knapsacks on their backs crammed with books. They counted two Frenchmen, two French-speaking Savoyards (but enemies of the French in this war), four Spanish subjects of Charles V, and one neutral Portuguese. To attract less attention they split into two groups. In French territory the Frenchmen did the talking. In German and Italian lands the Spaniards came forward. If soldiers questioned them on the first leg of their journey, they said they were students at the University of Paris making a pilgrimage to a

shrine near Strasbourg. While in France, they were frequently drenched with rain; they stayed at inns on the way
but were short on money and food. While tramping the
dirt roads they sometimes prayed silently, sometimes sang
the psalms together. Their trip started in November and
continued into January; December saw them crossing the
Alps. The warmth of Loyola's welcome when they reached
Venice on January 8 provided some compensation for the
cold of those mountains.

At Venice Loyola and his companions settled in the hospital of Saints John and Paul and the hospital of the Incurables, where they devoted themselves to helping the sick.
The incurables were mainly men dying from the venereal
disease syphilis, which Columbus's sailors seem to have
brought back to Europe from the New World. It swept Europe with a devastating effect similar to that of AIDS today. One of the companions, Simon Rodrigues, has left us
a description of their hospital work. They did menial
tasks, making beds and sweeping floors, cleaning utensils,
digging graves and burying the dead, and trying to cheer
up the patients as best they could. He relates how a patient
asked Xavier to rub his back, which was covered with running sores. Despite his nausea and fear of catching disease,
Xavier did as requested. Usually the companions found
satisfaction and joy in helping the sick and dying. Word of
what these Paris graduates, several of them noblemen,
were doing greatly impressed the Venetian elite.

The nine companions left Venice on May 16 and
reached Rome nine days later. They came seeking papal
permission for the group to make the pilgrimage to
Jerusalem. Loyola stayed in Venice because he feared that
two influential men at the papal court might try to block
papal approval. Earlier, Loyola had unpleasant encounters
with them. One was Carafa, who had recently been
named a cardinal. The other was Pedro Ortiz, who had
been a professor in Paris and had been angered when

Ignatius gave the Spiritual Exercises to one of his relatives. Ortiz had come to Rome to represent Charles V in defending the marriage of his aunt, Catherine of Aragon, against the efforts of Henry VIII to divorce her. Later he secured a place in the papal curia. Far from causing trouble for the companions, Ortiz secured them an audience with Paul III on 3 April 1537.

Traditionally popes have eaten alone. Paul III, who liked to have theologians debate while he dined, asked several of the companions to make presentations. He was so delighted by their performance that he not only gave them his blessing and permission for the pilgrimage but also donated sixty ducats for their expenses and encouraged other churchmen at Rome to contribute. As a result the nine returned with letters of credit for 260 ducats, about $100,000 in buying power today. At this point only Faber, Jay, and Broët were priests. Paul III also gave permission for six of them plus Ignatius to be ordained by any bishop and granted them extraordinary powers to absolve from heinous sins, powers usually restricted to bishops. Back in Venice Loyola, Xavier, Laínez, Rodrigues, Bobadilla, and Codure were ordained priests on 24 June 1535 by the bishop of Arbe, a small Venetian town. The ceremony was in his private chapel. Salmerón had to postpone his ordination for four months, till he reached twenty-two, the minimum age for ordination. Shortly before their ordination all the companions made vows of poverty and chastity.

After the companions returned to Venice, they again began caring for the sick in the hospitals while awaiting a ship to Palestine. Usually pilgrim ships left Venice in June, but in 1537 no pilgrim ship sailed, for the first time in thirty-eight years. War with the Turks was on the horizon. At this stage of the long rivalry between Charles V and the Ottoman sultan Suleiman the Magnificent, the emperor was the aggressor, having personally led a successful attack on Tunis in 1535. The Turkish fleet under Barbarossa blocked the exit from the Adriatic Sea into the Mediterranean, with disastrous results for Venetian trade. The imperial fleet, now under Andrea Doria, was skirmishing with Barbarossa off the heel of Italy. Venice was edging toward an alliance with the papacy and Charles V against the Turks, who were allied with the French. Earlier Charles V had sought an alliance with the shah of Persia, on the eastern flank of the Ottoman Empire; Suleiman replied to this by sending his army east and taking Baghdad and most of modern Iraq from the shah. War between Venice and Suleiman began in September 1537.

The Holy League, a formal alliance of the emperor, the pope and the Venetian Republic against the Turks, was concluded in 1538. But the Turks defeated the Venetian fleet at the Battle of Prevesa and in 1540 forced the Venetians to make peace. The Venetians had to surrender their last outpost in southern Greece and pay the Turks a heavy indemnity. Arguably this was a world war since there was fighting in Europe, Asia, and Africa, and the war had an enormous impact on the life of Loyola and his companions. Had they carried out their dream of going to Palestine, their missionary activities would almost certainly have incensed Turkish authorities. Most likely they would have ended up galley slaves in the Turkish fleet, or worse.

When it was clear that there would be no ship for the time being, the companions decided to work as priests in the region around Venice; that way, if a pilgrim ship became available, they could gather quickly to fulfill their vow and go to Jerusalem. They split into five groups. On July 25 Loyola went with Faber and Laínez to Vicenza, a Venetian possession to the west. There they settled into an abandoned monastery and devoted their first forty days to prayer since most of the companions were preparing to celebrate their first Mass. Ignatius did most of the cooking, while Faber and Laínez begged for food. During his years of study Loyola had sharply limited the amount of his prayer time, but during these forty days mystical experiences returned. In large measure he was reliving his spiritual experiences at Manresa fifteen years earlier.

After the forty days the companions went to the cities near Venice and began preaching in the town squares. Shouting and waving their hats, they gathered onlookers and the curious. Ignatius proved even slower than the rest at picking up Italian, but they did not let their bad Italian or the snickers from the crowd stop them. In fact, they found that their preaching touched many people, who often gave them alms. They also worked with the sick and poor.

All the companions, except for two who were ill, met at Vicenza in October 1537. Clearly their planned pilgrimage was out of the question, at least for a time. The vow they had taken on Montmartre at Paris to wait for a year was a bit unclear: did the clock start ticking in January of 1537 when they arrived in Venice or in June when the pilgrim ship usually left for Jerusalem? Regardless, they decided to await political developments for several more months before going to Rome and putting themselves at the Pope's disposal—the backup clause of their Montmartre vow. They decided meanwhile to disperse to Italian university towns. Loyola, Laínez, and Faber, probably at the suggestion of Pedro Ortiz, went to Rome; two each went to Padua, Ferrara, Bologna, and Siena. During their discussions a question arose: if people asked, what name or label should they give their group? They decided to say they were the *Compañia de Jesús,* the company or companions of Jesus. *Companions* literally means "those who eat bread [*panis* in Latin] together." In Latin the phrase became *Societas Iesu,* in English the *Society of Jesus.* In those days *compañia* and its French and Italian equivalents meant a loosely associated religious group more often than it did a business or military unit. The title *Company of Jesus* was later to stir intense opposition, for many people saw it as a sign of arrogance. The name *Jesuits* was soon coined as a term of contempt by their enemies, but gradually the companions came to accept it because it was short and convenient.

Loyola, Laínez, and Faber had to delay their journey to Rome to deal with new accusations that Loyola had fled Spain and Paris, where he had been burned in effigy. The vicar of the papal legate held a hearing that brought together both accusers and supporters of Ignatius and his companions. Ignatius was declared not guilty on 13 October 1537, and the accusations were dismissed as false and without foundation. Several weeks later the three began their trip to Rome.

About twelve miles from Rome on the road down from Siena lay the small dilapidated chapel of La Storta. The three stopped briefly to pray, and Loyola had a spiritual experience that profoundly moved him and gave him confidence that God was with him. He describes the experience in his autobiography, and we have accounts of it from Laínez, who was there, and from four other Jesuits who knew Ignatius well. Here is Loyola's description of the experience, written as was common in sixteenth-century autobiographies, in the third person: "One day, a few miles before they reached Rome, he was praying in a chapel and underwent so great a change in his heart and saw very clearly that God the Father was putting him with Christ his Son that he could not dare to have doubts about it." Laínez related that Ignatius heard in his heart the words from God "I will be favorable to you in Rome." Laínez adds that Loyola somehow experienced Christ carrying the cross, with God the Father saying to Christ, "I want you to take this man as your servant." Christ then said to Ignatius, "I desire you to serve us."

Regardless of how the modern reader may interpret this experience, it buoyed Ignatius and the other Jesuits who related the story. Years later, when they looked back, they saw in this experience a promise of divine help for the Jesuit Order. Initially, Ignatius was unsure of the experience's implications—the identification with Christ carrying a cross might mean that he and his companions would face opposition and troubles. He warned them to be very circumspect in their dealings with women lest these dealings provide ammunition for false accusations. Loyola in his autobiography notes that somewhat later in Rome both Xavier and Codure heard the confessions of two women involved in love affairs, which gave rise to suspicions—fortunately for the Jesuits the women's real male partners were discovered, and the two Jesuits were exonerated.

Loyola, Laínez, and Faber took up lodging in Rome near the church of Trinità dei Monti—today a tourist attraction at the top of the famous Spanish Steps. Faber and Laínez were assigned to lecture on theology at the University of Rome, then known as *La Sapienza,* from the palace that housed the lectures. Faber taught scripture while Laínez explained a scholastic treatise on the mass. As has been noted, Pope Paul III liked to listen to theology lectures during his meals, and Faber and Laínez were again invited to make presentations. Meanwhile Ignatius directed properly disposed people through the Spiritual Exercises. During Lent of 1538 he went down to Monte Cassino, the birthplace of Benedictine monasticism, to give the Exercises to Pedro Ortiz. It was the last time in his life that Ignatius traveled far from Rome and its surroundings. Ortiz profited greatly from the experience and testified that, although he was a veteran professor of sacred scripture, he had learned a new dimension from Loyola: how to apply theology to his daily living. It seems that during this period Ignatius may also have given the Exercises to Cardinal Gasparo Contarini, the leader of the cardinals and bishops who desired both to reform the Roman church and search for a possible theological reconciliation with Luther and other Protestant leaders. Two years later

Contarini went to Germany to deal with Protestant leaders at the Colloquy of Regensburg, sponsored by Emperor Charles V. Although they reached a tentative agreement on some doctrines, they made no progress on other disputed points, and the colloquy collapsed. Until his death in 1542 Contarini remained a friend and supporter of the Jesuits. While Loyola and Ortiz were returning from Monte Cassino, they encountered a young Spaniard, Francisco Estrada, who had just been dismissed from the service of Cardinal Carafa. At Rome Estrada made the Exercises and decided to join Ignatius and his companions. Later he became the most charismatic preacher among the early Jesuits.

During Lent of 1538 a crisis arose. Faber and Laínez were among those attending the sermons of the popular Augustinian friar Agostino Mainardi, who enjoyed the support not only of his audiences but also of important men in the papal government, including several Spaniards. His sermons presented a theology of grace drawn from the writings of Martin Luther. Faber and Laínez arranged a meeting and tried to persuade him to retract what he had been teaching. Mainardi not only refused, but counterattacked by having his Spanish friends launch a smear campaign against Loyola and his companions, accusing them of lacking morals and being heretics and Lutherans in disguise who had fled to Rome after having been investigated by the Inquisition in Spain, Paris, and Venice. Their accusations were backed up by Miguel de Landívar, who had been Xavier's personal servant in Paris. After Xavier came under Loyola's influence, he had dismissed Landívar, who blamed Loyola and determined to kill him in revenge. Seething with rage and carrying a knife in his hand, he mounted the stairs of the college looking for Loyola. Suddenly he met his intended victim, who addressed him. Stunned, Landívar stopped and fell to his knees. Years later he briefly joined the companions in Venice, then left.

He turned up later in Rome and wanted to join again but was rebuffed, probably because of his instability.

The rumors encouraged by Mainardi's friends and Landívar spread like wildfire, and people began to shun the three companions. Cardinal Gian Domenico De Cupis, dean of the College of Cardinals, believed the rumors and tried to persuade Quirino Garzoni, who had been hosting Ignatius and his two companions in his house, to throw them out. The cardinal claimed they were wolves in sheep's clothing, but Garzoni refused to budge. Ignatius reacted in his usual way. He obtained an audience with the cardinal; after two hours of discussion he so convinced the cardinal that he begged Loyola's pardon and became his supporter. De Cupis also obtained an audience for Loyola with the governor of Rome, Benedetto Conversini. There Loyola showed Conversini an old letter from Landívar that heaped praises on the companions. As a result Landívar was banished from Rome, and Conversini dropped all charges against Ignatius and his companions.

But rumors and accusations continued to circulate. Having the charges dropped did not satisfy Loyola; he wanted a legal vindication that would protect his companions and himself from future accusations. Hence they obtained letters praising their work from officials in Siena, Bologna, and Ferrara, where they had been preaching. Pope Paul III had just returned from Nice, in southern France, where he had helped broker a peace between Charles V and Francis I. Late in August of 1538 Loyola managed to get an hour-long audience with Paul III in his country villa at Frascati, just outside Rome. There he explained to the pope how he and his companions had been dogged by groundless accusations about their morals and orthodoxy; he asked the pope to appoint someone to conduct an investigation. The pope agreed. By a remarkable coincidence the judges who had been involved in previous investigations against Loyola at Alcalá, Paris, and Venice were in Rome at the time, and all three testified in Loyola's favor. So did Pedro Ortiz and other leading men. The governor of Rome pronounced the companions innocent of all charges in November of 1538. Loyola requested that the names of his accusers be dropped from the final verdict, but he had many copies of it made so they could be presented to officials in cities where hostile rumors circulated. In 1540 Mainardi fled Italy and became a successful Calvinist preacher in Italian-speaking areas of Switzerland.

In late April 1538 the other early companions of Ignatius left the university cities of northern Italy and gathered at Rome with Loyola, Faber, and Laínez to decide how they should proceed, now that it was clear that the pilgrimage to Jerusalem was impossible. On Christmas Eve Loyola celebrated mass for the first time—some eighteen months after his ordination as a priest. Having hoped that his first mass would be at Bethlehem, he chose the next best place: a chapel in the ancient Basilica of St. Mary Major that was thought to contain the manger where the infant Jesus had been placed at birth. His dream of working in Jerusalem was dead.

In October 1538 the companions occupied a large house near the center of Rome. The house was deserted because people thought it was haunted by ghosts, due to strange sounds heard after dark. Loyola's companions paid no heed to the noises and rumors. Very soon the house became a center for poor relief. The winter of 1538–1539 was extremely cold. Crops that fall had been very bad so that the price of grain soared. Poor people from the countryside flocked into Rome looking for food. Loyola and his companions visited wealthy cardinals and churchmen to beg alms to buy food for the poor, some three hundred of whom gathered most days at their doors. They also scrounged for firewood and places for poor people to sleep. They ministered to their spiritual poverty by giving catechism lessons in the largest room of the house and preaching and hearing confessions in nearby churches.

The companions carried out the fallback clause of their vow at Montmartre—to put themselves at the pope's disposal if they could not go to Jerusalem. Even earlier, when they had been holding a disputation at the papal dinner table, Paul III asked them why they were so eager to go to Jerusalem when there was so much work to be done for God in Italy. Their need to reach a decision on what to do with the rest of their lives was increased by demands on their services. The king of Portugal wanted to send trained priests to India; the Spanish ambassador wanted men for the Americas. Paul III had earmarked two companions to go to Siena and supervise the reform of a Benedictine convent of nuns. Similar requests could be expected. The companions would soon be freelancers scattered to the far corners of the globe unless they could build a structure for their friendship and collective identity in God's service: in short they would have to think about establishing a new religious order.

Loyola and his companions decided to continue their work during the day but to meet each night after supper and discuss different aspects and options of their plans. A decision was pressing, so they met regularly from March to June 1539. Each of them would reflect and pray over the options during the day but without discussing the question with the others before they met in common. Then each would present his arguments for or against that day's issue. Decisions were expected to be made by consensus. They easily agreed that they wanted somehow to stay together as a group, even if scattered in different locations. They were convinced that as an organized group they could work more effectively for God and lead more meaningful lives. They had already taken two of the three vows traditional in religious orders, poverty and chastity; should they now add the third vow of obedience? Without a vow of obedience, they realized, their band of companions would eventually break up. Should the vow be made to the pope or to one of their number whom they would elect as their superior? Since popes had so many other responsibilities and could not easily know the strengths and limitations of individuals in their group, the companions decided they must elect their own superior. These two decisions meant in effect that they would establish a new religious order.

The companions finished their deliberations on June 24. In fact, even before they finished their deliberations the pope had sent four of them on assignments to Siena, Parma, and Piacenza, in central Italy. Two more left the next month. Loyola was entrusted with the task of drawing up their proposals in five chapters called the Formula of the Institute so that their decisions could be presented to Paul III for approval. The Formula covered many topics: their collective name (the Society of Jesus); its purpose; the traditional three vows of poverty, chastity and obedience; and the special fourth vow, to go on missions when the pope requested this of individual Jesuits. The Formula discussed briefly the admission of new members and their training and the authority of the superior general of the order and renounced the sort of fixed incomes that the monastic orders had traditionally drawn from landholdings. On two points it differed sharply with the practice of earlier religious orders. First, priests did not recite together the divine office (the set prayers that usually took an hour to read privately but much longer to recite or sing together as a group). Loyola himself greatly enjoyed the chanting of the office, but chanting would tie Jesuits down and cut into their ability to travel, preach, hear confessions, and perform other tasks for the service of God and of their neighbors. Secondly, no physical penances, such as fasting or whipping oneself, were laid down by rule but were left to each individual's zeal and discretion. New members were not to be admitted permanently until they had demonstrated they could shoulder heavy responsibilities. Finally, the Formula stated a desire for a more detailed set of constitutions, which could be written only after the new order had gathered experience.

The good friend of the Jesuits, Cardinal Gasparo Contarini, asked Paul III to approve the Formula during midsummer. The pope turned the document over to his official theologian for study, who took two months before approving it. Then, again at Loyola's behest, Contarini read the Formula aloud to Paul III. On September 3 the pope gave his approval, saying, "The Finger of God is here." It appeared that Loyola and his companions had an open road before them.

Instead, they ran into a roadblock: the papal bureaucracy. The pope asked Cardinal Girolamo Ghinucci, in charge of papal letters or briefs, to drawn up a brief approving the new order. Ghinucci felt that the matter was too important for a mere brief and would require a formal papal bull, hence more investigation. He himself had three concrete difficulties with the Formula: the absence of a common recitation of office and of required physical penances, and the special vow of obedience to the pope to go on missions. Paul III solved the Ghinucci problem by turning the question over to Cardinal Bartolomeo Guidiccioni instead. But that made getting approval even more difficult: although Guidiccioni agreed with all the particulars in the Formula, he was opposed in principle to setting up any new religious orders. Indeed, he wanted the many existing religious orders to be amalgamated into four traditional ones. He rebuffed Loyola's attempts to meet and discuss the problem with him until the pope explicitly ordered him to do so. Meanwhile Loyola asked all the Jesuits to besiege heaven with their prayers and also urged many influential people throughout Italy to write Guidiccioni letters of recommendation for the new order. Finally

Guidiccioni yielded, but not without gaining a minor victory: the papal bull approving the Jesuits, *Regimini militantis Ecclesiae,* restricted the number of full or professed members of the Society of Jesus to sixty. Paul III issued the bull on 27 September 1540. A later papal bull (21 July 1550) reconfirmed the society and dropped the numerical restriction.

Now that the society had full status as a religious order, it had to elect a superior general. Of the original ten core members only three were in Rome. Three who were outside Italy on assignments had marked sealed ballots before leaving. Loyola summoned the other four in Italy to Rome to prepare a draft of preliminary constitutions and to elect a superior. Key points in the draft were that the Jesuits would wear the same cassock as parish priests, rather than a distinctive habit or uniform used by the older religious orders, and that their superior general would serve for life rather than for a set number of years. After three days of prayer for guidance, the election took place on April 5. Ignatius voted for whichever companion received the majority: all the others voted for him. Several voters stated they had voted for Ignatius because he was their true leader and had gathered them together since their days at Paris a decade earlier. This was certainly true, yet his health was not good. Laínez, Salmerón, and Faber were far better theologians. He was the worst linguist in the group; during their preaching at Rome he preached only in Spanish while all the others preached in Italian.

Regardless of the vote, Ignatius did not accept the outcome, because of his sinful youth. He begged the others to rethink their votes. Eight days later they voted again, with exactly the same outcome. Again Ignatius did not want to accept the office of superior general—now he would leave the decision to his Franciscan confessor. For three days Ignatius conferred with him, going over all his sins and physical ailments and trying to make the best case against his serving as superior general. On the fourth day, which happened to be Easter Sunday, the Franciscan told him that he would be resisting the will of God if he refused to serve as superior. Ignatius insisted that he put this in writing; his confessor sent his decision in a sealed envelope to Loyola's companions. On Tuesday, April 19, Ignatius accepted the office that would shape the rest of his life. The whole group walked to the Basilica of St. Paul outside the old walls of Rome and took the vows of the new order one by one before receiving communion from Ignatius. After mass they embraced one another with tears of joy and began walking to the other six main pilgrimage churches of Rome—no short stroll.

Even before Loyola's election as superior general, he and Jean Codure were given the task of drawing up a full set of constitutions for the new order—the first draft of 1541 has already been noted. But Codure died 29 August 1541, and pressing duties limited Loyola's work on the Constitutions during the next six years. Thereafter, work on the Constitutions moved ahead rapidly. The delay was probably fortunate because it was better to learn from the lived experience of the society before laying down hard and fast regulations.

VIII

The Spiritual Exercises

If Loyola's greatest accomplishment was founding the Jesuits, his second great achievement was developing and writing *The Spiritual Exercises.* No single point in his life is perfectly suited for discussing the Exercises. They grew out of his spiritual experiences at Manresa and the notes he kept during this time. We have seen that he helped people at Alcalá, such as Maria de la Flor, to work through a scaled-down version of those Manresa experiences. He was giving a full version of the Exercises to students at Paris, many of whom became his companions and whom he regarded as cofounders of the Society of Jesus. It was at Paris that Loyola made the last major addition to the Exercises, the Rules for Thinking with the Church, which have already been discussed. The Spiritual Exercises, the actual process of prayer and reflection usually taking some thirty days, should be distinguished from *The Spiritual Exercises,* the book in which Loyola gave suggestions or directions for those guiding or directing **exercitants** (the people making the Exercises) through those thirty days of prayer and spiritual renewal. Obviously the actual process and the book were closely linked. Even after publication of *The Spiritual Exercises* at Rome in 1548, Loyola continued to insert minor additions and corrections to his own written Spanish text almost to the time of his death.

The Exercises had two main purposes: to teach people to pray more effectively and to help people who were trying to reshape their lives to find and embrace what they saw as God's will for them. Often the two purposes supported each other. Many people used the Exercises to make an election, a decision to redirect one's life or profoundly reform it. The people making these Exercises during Loyola's lifetime were already committed believers. Normally they were expected to stop their usual work and move away from their regular home or lodging to a place where they would find more solitude for prayer and reflection, removed from distractions or contact with relatives, friends, and servants. The place might be a monastery or lodgings rented for the purpose.

The director, the experienced spiritual guide who was directing exercitants through the Exercises, would usually visit each exercitant daily and check on how the previous day's prayer had gone. The director would then outline the subject for prayer and reflection during the coming day. Central to this process would be five periods during most days, each about an hour long, for meditation or contemplation. The director was expected to craft meditations and contemplations to the needs of individual exercitants. The director's work was usually quite time-consuming and required considerable spiritual wisdom and psychological skill since the personalities and needs of exercitants would vary considerably.

The five meditations or contemplations were spaced out over the day; there was usually one around midnight, another shortly after rising, one in mid morning, and two in the afternoon. Exercitants were expected to reflect on the subject of their prayer before beginning it and to reflect later about the actual experience of their prayer and how they might improve the next time. Loyola suggested a set prayer at the start of each contemplation period. Most meditations contained a number of related ideas for the exercitant to reflect upon. The last five or ten minutes were to be a colloquy, that is, an intimate conversation with God, Jesus Christ, or Mary, his mother.

The Spiritual Exercises were divided into four time periods, called weeks, though they usually did not take seven days. Often the first two weeks would take eight days each, whereas the last two weeks could be shorter. Usually there was a day of repose and relaxation between the weeks. The director decided how much time was spent on each week, largely depending on the spiritual progress of the individual exercitant.

At the outset of the Exercises exercitants were required to ponder what Loyola called the Fundamental Principle: human beings were created to praise and serve God and thereby save their souls. All other things were created to help them attain that end. Therefore they should use all things insofar as they help them to that end by cultivating a balanced attitude toward wealth or poverty, good health or bad health, and all things created. From the perspective of eternity, poverty may be better for some individuals than wealth; bad health may provide a better opportunity for serving God than good health.

The exercitants then moved on to meditate on sin—the sin of the angels, of Adam and Eve, and of themselves—and the consequences of those sins. A meditation on hell follows in which Loyola moves from intellectual reflection to what he calls an "application of the senses"—exercitants must try to visualize the vast pit of hell, to hear the weeping of the damned, to smell the fumes and stench, to taste the tears, to feel the flames. They will then converse with Christ, thanking him for having kept them from hell. Each of these meditations was to be made several times. The number of meditations will be adapted "insofar as the exercitants' age, physical condition and temperament enable them to perform all five exercises or only some of them." Toward the end of the first week exercitants were expected to confess their sins to a priest, often all the sins of their whole life—thus putting their past behind them as they redirected their lives to the praise and service of God.

The bridge between the first and second week of the Exercises is the meditation on the earthly and the eternal king. This meditation first describes an earthly king who invites knights to join him on a crusade in which they would share his hardships and triumphs, the meditation implying that anyone who would refuse such a noble invitation is a coward. Loyola then presents Christ as the eternal king who invites exercitants to join his enterprise and even his suffering for the spiritual good of themselves and others so that one day they might share his glory. Christ has won the definitive victory over evil, but he invites all men and women to share the struggle for the salvation of themselves and their fellow men and women. Every generous soul will embrace this invitation and challenge. Most of the other meditations of the second week center on the events of Christ's life from his incarnation and birth through his public life in Galilee and Judea. Ignatius invites exercitants to recreate in their imagination all the details in the events of the Gospels, even as a movie director has to work out the concrete details of a scene—setting, dialogue, interaction and movement of the actors. Ignatius himself had an intense interest in the concrete details of Christ's life—recall how in Jerusalem he went back to see how Christ's feet were thought to have faced at his ascension. The purpose of these inward re-creations of events in Christ's life is to help exercitants know him more intimately and follow him more closely. They are to assimilate his values and make them their guide through life.

On the fourth day of the second week, exercitants made the Meditation on the Two Standards. This presents two leaders, Satan and Christ, trying to rally armies to their standards (the equivalent to flags in the Roman army). Satan tries to allure recruits first to wealth, then honor, and finally to pride, from which all other vices flow. Christ encourages his followers to embrace poverty and humility as the basis of acquiring all the other virtues. The Meditation on the Two Standards ends with exercitants engaging in three short conversations with Mary, Jesus, and God the Father in which they beg that they may be enrolled under Christ's banner and forsake any quest for worldly riches and honors.

Loyola spells out in some detail several meditations on Christ's public life, but usually he gives only a short reference to events and passages in the Gospels that the director was expected to pick out and develop as he judged best for the individual exercitant. Exercitants were expected to repeat all the major meditations of the Exercises several times, and they often had to repeat even less important meditations once.

Loyola often gave the Exercises to people who were considering making an election. At the end of the second week, these exercitants made their election (or concrete decision) about how they were going to restructure the rest of their lives. To give several examples, the decision might be to enter a religious order, or to marry, or to increase the role of prayer in one's life, or to earmark major funds for helping the poor. For people making an election the last two weeks of the Exercises centered on confirming their election. Loyola devotes four full pages of *The Spiritual Exercises* to guidelines for making a good election. He suggests three ways or times. The first occurs when, thanks to divine inspiration, one feels utterly convinced that a given course of action is God's will. The second occurs when the different experience of joy or anxiety in prayer suggests the better choice of action. The third way is to line up the reasons for and against a certain choice and then evaluate the opposing reasons in the light of the

Fundamental Principle—what leads most to God's glory and one's eternal salvation. Alternatively, one can stand aside and ask, "What advice would I give a person I do not know who came for my advice on this choice?" or "On my deathbed or at the Day of Judgment what choice would I wish I had made?"

The third week centers on the last days of Christ's life, especially the Last Supper with his disciples, his hearings before Jewish and Roman officials, and his condemnation, crucifixion, death, and burial. Although exercitants are to picture the sufferings of Christ, more important than his physical pain are his interior sufferings and the exercitants' recognition that he endured all this for each one of them.

The mood of the fourth week is joy, and the meditations ponder the apparitions of the risen Jesus from Easter till his ascension into heaven. The number of meditations is cut from five to four per day. The last meditation of the Spiritual Exercises is entitled "A Contemplation for Achieving Love." Ignatius begins it by observing that love should be expressed by actions rather than words. Love consists in sharing what one has with the beloved. The purpose of the contemplation is "a heartfelt appreciation of all the blessings God has given me so that, fully grateful, I may become completely devoted to God in effective love." Exercitants then reflect on all of God's gifts to them—"how much God has done for me, how much that is His Own He has shared with me." In return exercitants are to offer all they have and all they are to God. They are to see God living in His creatures, giving them existence, life, intelligence—"giving me too my existence, life, consciousness, intelligence, . . . making me His temple." The meditation then reflects on how God works in all created reality and how all human abilities and virtues flow from God "like sunbeams from the sun or streams from their source." The Contemplation for Achieving Love strikes a more mystical note than the rest of the Exercises and invites exercitants to a higher level of reflection and prayer.

It is important to stress that the Exercises center on Christ—the last three weeks follow his life as it is related in the Gospels. Many Christian spiritual writers of the Reformation centered on God as omnipotent creator, meanwhile tending to neglect how God's plan for women and men is revealed in Christ. Their approach was often hard for ordinary people of the sixteenth century to relate to, much less to meditate on, as compared to the Gospel stories that Loyola invited people to recreate in their imagination. Many commentators have also noted that the Spiritual Exercises do not simply present a diverse collection of meditations; rather they progress logically and psychologically from the Fundamental Principle through the life of Christ to the lofty Contemplation for Achieving Love of God. If one scrambles the order of meditations in the Exercises, they lose much of their impact and cohesion.

As noted at the beginning of this chapter, there is no one best point in Loyola's life to discuss the Spiritual Exercises. By 1548 many Jesuits were directing people through the Exercises, using handwritten notes and directives. Clearly a printed edition would save the work of multiplying handwritten copies and make for a more faithful and precise use of the Exercises. Some prominent theologians, especially in Spain, were alarmed by rumors they had heard about the Exercises. Loyola wanted to counter any rumors about brainwashing. He handwrote his own copy of the Exercises in Spanish and kept making minor additions. That Spanish copy is the source of modern editions and translations. There also was an early Latin translation, perhaps by Loyola himself, but it lacked polish. Loyola was well aware of his own limitations in writing Latin. He turned to one of the Jesuits at Rome noted as a fine Latin stylist, the Frenchman André des Freux, and had him make an eloquent Latin translation—but one that missed a few nuances of Loyola's own Spanish text. Loyola had the Latin translations submitted to Pope Paul III for official approval; the pope issued a public letter praising the Exercises on 31 July 1548. In September *The Spiritual Exercises* in des Freux's Latin translation was published in Rome in a limited edition of some five hundred copies—limited because the text was not meant to be sold to the public or even read by people making the Exercises. It was a manual or guidebook for the directors who were guiding exercitants. Most of the directors would be Jesuit priests, but Loyola believed that only a minority of Jesuits would have the spiritual wisdom and psychological skills needed to serve effectively as directors.

The Spiritual Exercises went on to be a phenomenal success—it has enjoyed continuous use from 1548 up to the present and has been translated into all the world's major languages. It is a short book, about one hundred pages long. Unlike most books that enjoy long-lasting success, *The Spiritual Exercises* is a bad read. Anyone who tries to read the book cover to cover will find it to be a labyrinth. Most sections are clear enough; Loyola could be clear and precise as a writer but rarely eloquent. The British scholar A. G. Dickens has observed about the *Exercises,* "The craving of a troubled but order-seeking century was a craving for precise guidance, and this Loyola offered." The Exercises were not intended to be read but to be experienced. One cannot judge the value of a book on physical exercises by reading the it—one must do the exercises. Nor can one rate a cookbook by reading it—one must follow the recipes, do the cooking, and savor the meal before passing judgment. The same is true for *The Spiritual Exercises,* and this is doubtless one reason why Loyola himself ordered Jesuits not to give a copies to people who had not yet made the Exercises.

We have already glanced at some of the major meditations and the overall structure of the Spiritual Exercises, but these occupy only about half the book's pages. The rest of the book covers rules and advice for the director of the Exercises to share or not with exercitants, depending on their individual needs. Let us look at some of these. The book begins not with the first meditation but with twenty annotations or observations as to how the director should deal with the needs of different exercitants. Immediately after the first meditation come nineteen directions on how to make an examination of conscience, a practice that Loyola valued highly. This is followed by some suggestions about receiving the sacraments of confession and communion. At the end of the first week, Loyola adds suggestions on how to prepare for the meditations as well as recommendations on eating and sleeping habits during the retreat. There are also suggestions on how to make certain meditations or contemplations more effective: for instance, will darkening my room or going for a walk outside in the sun or doing physical penances help me to pray better? Loyola suggests that perhaps elderly or weaker exercitants should not make meditations in the middle of the night.

In addition to the meditations, Loyola provides rules and suggestions on many ways to improve one's life. Thus he gives twenty rules or recommendations for exercitants who might be making an election about changing their state in life or reforming it. During the third week, there are rules for developing healthy eating habits. After the fourth week, there are several appendices: on almsgiving, on overcoming scruples, and on three ways of praying. In all, the Spiritual Exercises teach six ways of praying. Loyola was convinced that people making the Exercises would experience special graces from God but also temptations arising from their own sinful inclinations or from the devil. In tempting devout people, Loyola argued, the devil is too clever to rely on crass temptations—he comes as an angel of light. How could exercitants distinguish the workings of God in their hearts from temptations? Loyola gives directors two sets of rules to help discern the difference and help exercitants do the same. Directors are to teach the first set during the first week. The second set is more subtle, and directors are to teach these rules only when the exercitants seem more spiritually advanced and their temptations are more subtle.

Earlier we observed that the Spiritual Exercises evolved over the course of Loyola's life from his conversion experience to his death. The most important single source of experience from which the Exercises were drawn seems to have been his reflections on his own spiritual growth at Manresa. His studies at Paris added theological depth. Efforts to find echos of previous spiritual writings in the text of the *Exercises* have had mixed results. Obviously there are many references to the Bible, especially to the Gospels. The deep inwardness of Loyola's favorite postbiblical book, *The Imitation of Christ* by Thomas à Kempis, is pervasive even if direct quotations are not. Scholars are not agreed, however, about the influence of some medieval spiritual writers.

The experience that Loyola and his Paris companions gained from actually directing people through the Exercises led Loyola to modify some things he had done at Paris. There he seems to have encouraged his companions to fast severely and do physical penances during the first days of the Exercises. As noted earlier, Peter Faber made the Exercises in an unheated room during the dead of winter and went six days without any food before Loyola discovered what he was doing and put a stop to it lest he injure his health. Faber's actions were generous but unwise. Xavier also went too far in physical penances and had to be stopped. The text of the later printed *Spiritual Exercises* urges caution in doing penance.

Gradually more people came forward to make the Exercises, but directing a person through the full thirty days with daily conferences could be very time-consuming for the handful of Jesuit priests who were skilled directors. Three solutions, none fully satisfactory, were tried. One way used by the early Jesuits was to conduct a retreat based on the Exercises for a group of people, for instance to a whole monastery. But this did not allow for the close, individualized direction and shaping of the various meditations that Ignatius had originally intended. Regardless, this is the way that the Exercises were usually given from roughly 1570 to 1970. Since 1970 there has been an increase in the original one-on-one relation between director and exercitant. A second way, approved by Ignatius with some misgivings, arose when a whole convent of nuns requested the Exercises. A gifted nun was selected; after she had made the full thirty-day retreat under a Jesuit, she was given a copy of the *Exercises*. She then directed the other nuns in her convent one by one through the Exercises. A third method was to give an abbreviated version of the Exercises, often eight days and concentrating on the first week. Loyola recommended this method for persons who seemed less gifted spiritually and less likely to make a decision or election that would reshape their future lives.

As has been seen, initially many people making the Exercises were considering an election about a state in life, but later Loyola himself and his companions directed persons who had already made life commitments—for instance, married persons or churchmen—through the complete process. In Loyola's time, men who entered the Jesuits (called novices) often made the full Exercises, but those who had made them before entering either were not required to repeat them or did so only in an abbreviated form. Later, all novices were required to make the full Exercises. The Exercises proved an important recruiting tool that led many young men who made them to enter the early Jesuits.

The full impact of *The Spiritual Exercises* is impossible to measure, but the fact that more than 5,000 editions have been printed since 1548 suggests the book's enormous influence. During the late sixteenth and early seventeenth centuries, books of systematic meditation enjoyed great popularity among both Catholics and Protestants. Many of these books came from the pens of Jesuits and spread the prayer techniques taught in the Exercises. Here let us mention just one such Jesuit author who is now virtually forgotten, the Spaniard Luis de La Puente (1554–1624). Among his works was *Meditations on the Mysteries of Our Holy Faith,* which follows the same order as the Exercises. The English edition (London, 1852) was in six volumes. More than 260 editions were published; it was especially popular in seventeenth-century France.

IX

"To Go to All Parts of the World"

As we have seen, the early Jesuits took a vow to accept any mission the pope might send them on, "either to the Turks or other unbelievers, even those who live in the parts called the Indies, or among heretics or schismatics or any of the faithful." The papal bulls of both 1540 and 1550, which authorized the Jesuits, repeated this statement of purpose. The Constitutions conferred on the superior general the power of assigning Jesuits to any part of the world. Right from the beginning, foreign missions became a major focus of Jesuit work, and they remain so today. When the King of Portugal wrote to Loyola in August 1546 encouraging the Jesuits to work in Ethiopia, Loyola wrote back, "I offer myself most willingly to you, in case [other Jesuits] do not wish to accept this work in Ethiopia."

The first Jesuit mission outside Italy was to Ireland. Paul III assigned Paschase Broët and Alfonso Salmerón to investigate the situation of Irish Catholics. They were named nuncios (papal ambassadors) and given sweeping powers. Henry VIII had broken with the papacy in 1536, when the pope would not grant him a divorce so that he could marry Anne Boleyn. This led many Irish Catholics, who resented English rule, to revolt, but Henry VIII's army had crushed all opposition by late 1541, when the two Jesuit nuncios left Rome. Before their departure Loyola gave them instructions on how to deal with people of various social ranks. They should listen willingly but speak little. With the vivacious they should be cheerful; with the slow to speak they too should be reticent. With people who were sad they should be cheerful, to counter their depression. In everything they should strive to win people to God's greater service.

The mission turned out an utter failure. At Lyons, in France, on their way north, Broët and Salmerón encountered Cardinal David Beaton of Scotland, who warned them that Henry VIII controlled all the Irish towns and castles and that the Irish were "of all mankind the wildest people, barbarians incapable of any discipline." The two Jesuits planned to sail from Belgium to Scotland, but twice storms forced their ship to land in England, where they had to hide for weeks from English authorities. In Scotland King James V welcomed them, but they could get little reliable information about Ireland. Their contacts in Scotland warned them to forget about venturing to Ireland because the Irish chiefs had surrendered to Henry and the Irish who remained loyal to Rome had fled to the hills. Still the Jesuits persisted and crossed Scotland from Edinburgh to Glasgow, where they found a ship that took them to Ireland. There they spent thirty-four days, during which their expectations about the future of Catholicism in Ireland sank still lower. When they returned to Scotland, people were amazed that they had made it back alive. When they reached Lyons, they looked so disheveled that they were thrown into prison as spies. Later Broët served ten years as the provincial superior of France, and Salmerón was provincial superior of Naples and southern

Italy for seventeen years, in addition to writing biblical commentaries.

In contrast to the failure of the mission to Ireland was the sterling work of Saint Francis Xavier (1506–1552) in Asia. Vasco da Gama's voyage to India in 1498 had laid the cornerstone of a Portuguese empire in the Far East; in fact the empire was a string of trading posts stretching along the coasts of Africa, India, and Indonesia plus links to Japan and China. The trading posts, backed by a navy enjoying superior technology, gave the Portuguese mastery of the seas between Asia and Europe until the Dutch seized control of the trade routes in the late sixteenth century. King John III of Portugal asked Paul III to send two Jesuits as missionaries to India. Loyola assigned Simon Rodrigues and Nicolás Bobadilla to the task, but Bobadilla fell ill, and Francis Xavier was the only other Jesuit priest available. When Loyola asked him whether he would be willing to go, Xavier replied, "Sure, right away. Here I am." Two days later he departed with the entourage of the Portuguese ambassador, never to see Loyola again. Rodrigues and Xavier reached Lisbon in June 1540, where their preaching enjoyed great success. The King was drawn to Rodrigues, a suave Portuguese nobleman, and kept him in Portugal to open a school. Rodrigues soon became tutor to the King's son and the superior of the fastest growing province (or administrative unit) of the Jesuits.

As Xavier was boarding the ship for India, he was handed papers making him a papal nuncio and a royal official. On the long voyage around Africa, ships were at the mercy of the winds, and Xavier's voyage stretched from April 1541 to May 1542. For almost half a year he preached at Goa, Portuguese headquarters in India, then moved to India's southeastern coast, where, helped by native catechists and interpreters, he confirmed the faith of 20,000 Christian converts among the pearl fishermen. It is claimed that he also baptized 10,000 people there.

Loyola sends Francis Xavier to India.

In 1545 he pushed on to the Portuguese trading center at Malacca, near modern Singapore. The next year he worked in the Moluccas, known as the Spice Islands, in modern Indonesia. He returned in mid-1547 to Malacca and then back to Goa, where he assigned newly arrived Jesuits to mission work, including the administration of a college at Goa. At Malacca, Xavier had encountered a Japanese nobleman named Anjiro who wanted to become a Christian. This man so impressed Xavier that he decided to explore the prospects of missionary work in Japan. Since no Portuguese dared take him there, Xavier hired a pirate and arrived in August 1549 at Kagoshima, Anjiro's hometown. There the local warlord gave Xavier permission to preach Christianity. Xavier was enormously impressed by the Japanese, whose literacy rate surpassed that of most European nations. After preaching with only mixed success in several Japanese cities never previously visited by Europeans, Xavier tried a new tactic. He and a Jesuit companion went to the palace of the warlord of Yamaguchi, Japan's most powerful ruler, and obtained permission to preach Christianity in Japan. They came clad not in their usual worn black cassocks but in colorful silk robes and gave the warlord gifts from Europe, including a clock, a music box, and mirrors. These changes were significant because they foreshadowed the willingness of future Jesuit missionaries, most notably in China, to accommodate to local thinking and customs. Later many non-Jesuit missionaries bitterly criticized such accommodations. Xavier also showed the warlord his credentials as an ambassador from the pope and from the king of Portugal. The warlord granted Xavier a decayed monastery to live in, and the city elite began to visit the two Jesuits. In six months they made five hundred converts. Soon Xavier returned again to Malacca and India to supervise the work of newly arrived Jesuits. In 1552 he set out again, this time hoping to penetrate China and sound out missionary prospects there, even though the Chinese emperor had forbidden Europeans to enter China. Xavier settled on a tiny island near Canton where he hoped to persuade some Chinese smugglers to sneak him onto the mainland. On the island he fell ill and died in December 1552. A major reason for his decision to try converting the Chinese was that many Japanese, who owed much of their culture to China, objected that Christianity could not be true if it was unknown to the Chinese.

In 1555 a catalogue of Jesuits working in the Orient was published at Goa and listed seventy-eight men: seven assigned to Ethiopia, ten in Indonesia, twelve in Japan, three at Ormuz, and the rest in India, where they were running four small schools. Their numbers were to grow in the coming decades. In 1622 the Catholic Church canonized Xavier along with Loyola, his old college roommate.

Xavier's impact back in Europe was almost as important as his actual work in Asia. He wrote letters to Loyola and to officials in Portugal that described his work and the people he was encountering. His letters were circulated widely. One of them criticized his old professors at Paris for spending their years at ease when there was enormous need for missionaries. His letters led many young men to volunteer for missionary work, sometimes as Jesuits, sometimes as Dominican or Franciscan friars. The second half of the sixteenth century was a golden age of Catholic missionary work in Asia and the Americas. The rise of the Ottoman Turkish empire in the fifteenth century had blocked most European contacts with Asia, but Spanish and Portuguese explorations and colonies now opened whole new countries and continents to missionary work. During the first half of the sixteenth century the success of the Protestant Reformation in winning whole nations away from Rome made Catholics defensive and discouraged, but that changed gradually after 1550 as news of Catholic missionary work spread. Proponents of the missions argued that the Roman church may have lost England, Scandinavia, and most of Germany and Switzerland to Protestantism but Catholicism was gradually sinking roots in Asia, Africa, and the Americas that would compensate for losses in Europe. By the end of the century the Catholic Church was well on its way to becoming a worldwide church.

Several recent studies have argued that the Jesuits played a central role in the exchange of culture and

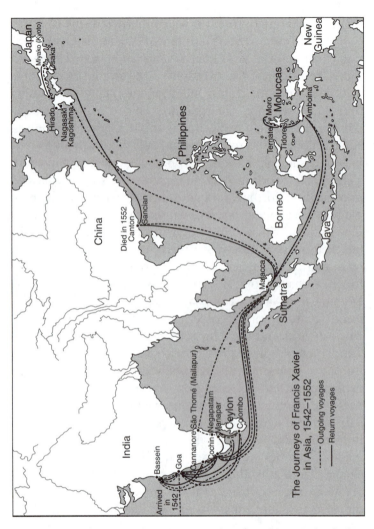

Francis Xavier's missionary journeys in Asia from his arrival in India in 1542 till his death just off the coast of China in 1552. Xavier was the first and greatest Jesuit missionary. He worked in India, Malaysia, Indonesia, and Japan. Adapted from the Institute of Jesuit Sources, St. Louis, MO, from the inside cover of *The Letters and Instructions of Francis Xavier,* translated by M. Joseph Costelloe (St. Louis: Institute of Jesuit Sources, 1992).

knowledge around the world. Loyola required that Jesuit communities send reports on their work to Rome at least every four months. His purpose was not only to keep the Jesuit headquarters in Rome well informed but also to provide information that the Jesuits could share with benefactors, both churchmen and laypeople, to win support for missionary work. Toward the end of the sixteenth century the Jesuits started publishing these reports, in part to win support for their missions. The Jesuits sent to distant places were better educated than the sailors, soldiers, and merchants who set out for Asia and the Americas. They had reason to study the governments, cultures, and religions they encountered and send reports back to prepare future missionaries. These reports have enormous value for historians today. The first such reports are the letters of Francis Xavier. Antonio Possevino (1533–1611) sent Pope Gregory XIII lengthy accounts of conditions in Scandinavia, Transylvania, and the Russia of Ivan the Terrible. The seventy-three volumes of the *Jesuit Relations,* reports by French Jesuit missionaries in Canada and the Mississippi region between 1632 and 1673, are an unrivaled source of information about native Americans in the seventeenth century.

Matteo Ricci (1552–1610) not only penetrated China but became a favorite of the emperor at Beijing and shared with Chinese scholars his considerable knowledge of Western science and philosophy. His journals, which describe China and his work there, were published shortly after his death and gave Europeans their best view thus far of the most populous and powerful nation on earth. Loyola set up a number of confraternities in Rome to help people with various needs. Ricci and the Jesuits in China followed his example; their first Christian confraternities were set up in Beijing in 1609 and Nanjing in 1610. China had its own long tradition of benevolent societies, many of them also providing discussion forums for intellectuals.

While the Jesuit-sponsored confraternities in China built on this tradition, they put more stress on prayer and helping the poor. By the mid-1660s there were some four hundred Jesuit-sponsored devotional confraternities in China.

Asia was the main scene of early Jesuit foreign missionary work, but during Loyola's lifetime, efforts were made to establish beachheads in Brazil, the Congo, and Ethiopia. During his years at Rome he received appeals from three different bishops in Mexico who hoped for helpers in the daunting task of converting native Americans, but Jesuit work in Spanish America would have to wait two decades. Early in 1549 six Jesuits did leave Lisbon for Portuguese Brazil; after two months at sea they landed at Bahia and began work on three interlocking tasks: serving as pastors for the Portuguese colonists, preaching to native Americans, and teaching children. By 1553 there were thirty Jesuits in Brazil scattered through six towns. The Jesuits at Piratininga set up the College of Sao Paulo; later the town adopted the name of the college and today is the largest city in South America.

Jesuit efforts in Africa were less successful than in Asia and Brazil. A mission to the Congo (modern Zaire) never got beyond the planning stage. Far more promising was Ethiopia, where black Africans had accepted Christianity in the fourth century from Egyptian missionaries. During the Middle Ages many Europeans eagerly accepted the legend of Prester John, a mythical Christian ruler in the Middle East who had defeated Muslim kings. Later Europeans identified the Christian rulers of Ethiopia as successors of Prester John and hence saw them as potential allies in their struggle against the expanding Ottoman Empire. In fact, during Loyola's lifetime Islam was spreading into black Africa, and the Christian kings of Ethiopia, far from being able to help the West, were themselves in desperate need of Portuguese help. Yet this very need of help could be used to leverage a union of the Ethiopian church with Rome.

Loyola as Superior General of the Jesuits

Loyola's work as superior general of the Jesuits consumed most of his time and energy from his election in 1541 till his death in 1556. At his death there were a thousand Jesuits, and their numbers tripled in the next ten years. During the Reformation some twenty new male religious orders were founded; only the Capuchins (a reformed branch of the Franciscans) grew more rapidly, but a papal decree restricted them to Italy until 1574. The other new religious orders grew slowly and often flourished in only one country. There were many proposals that the small new orders should joined together since they shared many values and ministries. Two of these smaller orders approached the Jesuits and requested a union. One was Carafa's Theatines, who were founded in Rome and received papal approval in 1524 but by 1550 had only twenty-seven members. The other was the Somaschi, who were founded in Venice in 1534 and received papal approval in 1540, the same year as the Jesuits; they too grew only slowly. In both cases Loyola turned down proposed mergers because differences in spirituality and lifestyle were likely to cause friction.

A key factor in Jesuit growth was the fact that from the beginning the Jesuits were international. As we have seen, they began with a group of like-minded students at Paris and its international university. Most of the companions who joined Loyola in Venice to seek passage to the Holy Land were Spaniards (Xavier, Laínez, Salmerón, Bobadilla, and Diego de Hoces), but they also included a Portuguese (Rodrigues), two French-speaking Savoyards (Faber and Jay), and two Frenchmen (Broët and Codure). All the Spaniards except Xavier spent most of their later lives in Italy. Faber worked in Italy, Germany, and Spain. Broët preached in the cities of northern Italy until Loyola named him first the provincial superior of Italy, then, in 1552, provincial superior of France. He died assisting plague victims in Paris in 1562. Jay worked in Italy till 1542 and then in Germany till his death in 1552. Rodrigues returned to his native Portugal in 1541; his early success there was followed by a disaster which will be examined shortly. The previous chapter traced Xavier's missionary career in Asia.

As general of the Society of Jesus Loyola relied greatly on his early companions. All made important contributions to the growth and administration of the society, except Hoces and Codure, who died in 1538 and 1541, respectively. By Loyola's death in 1556 the Jesuits had been divided in eleven provinces, each under a regional superior called the provincial. The provinces were established in this order: Portugal, Spain (in 1554 Spain was split into three provinces, Aragon, Castile, and southern Spain), India, Italy, Sicily, Brazil, France, southern Germany, and northern Germany. Rome itself remained directly under Loyola. Since mail was slow and unreliable, direct and detailed control from Rome was impossible. The provincials enjoyed considerable discretion in making decisions, partly because the Jesuit Constitutions were only gradually being written and promulgated. Nevertheless, provincial superiors looked to Rome and Loyola for guidance. Loyola regarded his early companions as cofounders of the Jesuits, and Xavier, Rodrigues, Broët, Laínez, and Salmerón served as provincials. Bobadilla was always a maverick, but still he did marvelous work in reforming convents and preaching. He worked in no less than seventy different dioceses, mainly in southern Italy. After Xavier and Loyola himself, the most respected and beloved of Loyola's companions was Peter Faber, whose work took him to France, Germany, Spain, and Italy, where he died of exhaustion at age forty in 1546. Except for Ignatius himself, no one was better than Faber in directing people through the Spiritual Exercises.

Rarely does a person have an impact on history without the help of gifted friends and subordinates. Loyola's early companions played crucial roles in Jesuit history, but four men who joined the Jesuits in the 1540s were equally important: Peter Canisius, Francis Borgia, Juan Polanco, and Jerome Nadal. All were gifted, but in different ways.

Saint Peter Canisius (1521–1597) was a Dutchman who studied at the University of Cologne until 1541, when he learned about the work Peter Faber was doing up the Rhine River at Mainz. Canisius went to see Faber and made the Spiritual Exercises under his direction. He wrote a friend that he could hardly describe how the Exercises had transformed his life and made him a new man. He claimed that he had never encountered a theologian so learned or a man so virtuous as Faber. He then entered the Jesuits. Canisius was the first Jesuit to publish books— editions of the medieval mystic Johann Tauler and of Saint Cyril, the fifth-century bishop of Alexandria. In 1547 Canisius served briefly as theological advisor at the Council of Trent. Loyola then called him to Rome for spiritual training, which included washing dishes and scrubbing floors in the Jesuit residence and tending the sick at a hospital. Loyola next sent him to teach in Sicily at the first

Jesuit college for lay students. From 1549 to 1580 he worked in Bavaria and Austria as preacher, theology professor, university administrator, and writer; he was also the first provincial superior of the South German Province.

Canisius wrote three catechisms (one each for children, students, and adults), all similar in structure but with increasing length and sophistication. They remained popular in Germany for three centuries and were translated into twelve languages. Right from the start the Jesuits had made teaching catechism to children a priority, but Catholics were slow to publish catechisms that were as effective as Luther's. Canisius filled that need. His catechisms never mentioned Luther or Calvin by name and did not attack their teachings directly, but Canisius did stress Catholic doctrine on disputed questions such as justification and the sacraments. His catechisms also stressed the need to live a virtuous and devout life. Canisius played a role second to none in the revitalization of German Catholicism during the crucial years 1550 to 1600.

Saint Francis Borgia (1510-1572) was the grandson of the notorious Renaissance pope Alexander VI and of King Ferdinand of Aragon. His father was duke of Gandia, in southern Spain, and Francis inherited his dukedom. He held important offices in the administration of Emperor Charles V before the death of his wife in 1546. Shortly before her death Borgia had met Peter Faber and other Jesuits who made a deep impression on him. After making a retreat he decided to become a Jesuit, but he could not simply resign as duke. He had eight children, for whom he had to arrange inheritances, dowries, and marriages. He wrote Loyola about his desire to become a Jesuit. Loyola agreed to accept him but told him to keep his plans secret. He secretly made the first vows of a Jesuit in 1548 but continued to live like a duke while studying theology. Two years later the miniuniversity he had founded at Gandia awarded him a doctorate in theology. It is hard to imagine a professor giving the duke a failing grade.

During the Jubilee Year of 1550 Borgia made a pilgrimage to Rome and brought along some twenty-five nobles and servants to conceal his real purpose: to meet Loyola and arrange his official entrance into the Jesuits. He returned to Spain and resigned his dukedom to his son Carlos. As soon as Charles V ratified his resignation, Borgia donned clerical garb. He was ordained a month later, in May 1551. Loyola had predicted that the news of Borgia's entering the Jesuits would cause an explosion. It did. For a man of such wealth and distinction to embrace a life of poverty, chastity, and obedience astonished many people. Crowds flocked to hear his sermons. In 1554 Loyola put him in charge of all Jesuits in Spain and Portugal. Within a few years he founded twenty colleges in Spain, where growth of the Jesuits had initially been slower than in Portugal or Italy but now increased rapidly. After the death of Loyola and Laínez, Borgia served as the third general of the Jesuits from 1565 to 1572.

Jerome Nadal (1507–1580) was born on the island of Majorca, off Spain's Mediterranean coast. He studied at Alcalá and the University of Paris, where Ignatius quickly recognized his talent and piety. When he fell ill Ignatius visited him in the hospital and subsequently took walks with him, but Nadal rebuffed Loyola when he invited Nadal to join his companions. Nadal feared that Ignatius and his companions would eventually run afoul of the Inquisition. Later Nadal returned to Spain and was ordained a priest, but he found little satisfaction in his work. Then he was deeply moved by a letter in which Francis Xavier described missionary work in India. Nadal went to Rome in 1543 and asked Loyola to accept him as a Jesuit. Gradually Loyola began to see that Nadal had an exceptional feel for the evolving work and spirit of the new order and began entrusting to him important tasks such as running the first Jesuit college for lay students at Messina, in Sicily. Later he was charged with setting up three other Jesuit communities in Sicily. He also wrote the first Jesuit treatise on education. When he was chaplain for Spanish troops sailing from Sicily to Africa, his ship sank and his Jesuit companion was drowned, but Nadal was rescued and did hospital work among the troops in Africa. Loyola later sent him to explain and promulgate the Jesuit Constitutions in Spain, Portugal, and Germany. The historian James Brodrick says of this work, "One almost gets dizzy in trying to keep pace with him as he tramps or rides or sails from one end of Europe to the other, carrying to the far-flung Society of Jesus the spirit and comfort of its Founder." Loyola also used him as a fundraiser for Jesuit colleges. After Loyola's death Laínez entrusted him with overseeing Jesuit work in France, Germany, Austria, Bohemia, and Poland.

Canisius, Borgia, and Nadal were men in motion, dealing with the problems and princes of many lands. Juan Polanco (1517–1576) served as Loyola's secretary and chief of staff during the last eight years of Loyola's life and was anchored in Rome during those crucial years. He was born in Burgos to a wealthy Jewish family that had converted to Catholicism. After studying humanities and philosophy at Paris he secured a position in the papal bureaucracy. After he made the Spiritual Exercises and entered the Jesuits, Loyola sent him to Padua to study theology. In 1547 he was appointed Loyola's secretary. In this seemingly secondary post he quickly became Loyola's right hand so that historians have called him Loyola's alter ego. Polanco was even better organized than Loyola and was a more gifted writer in Latin, Spanish, and Italian—the three languages most used at the Jesuit headquarters in Rome.

In the sixteenth century the most important way to organize the work of Jesuits, solve problems, and cultivate powerful benefactors was by letters. Most of Loyola's waking hours during his last decade must have been spent writing letters and instructions. Only 173 of Loyola's 6,816 surviving letters come from before Polanco's appointment as secretary in May 1547—all the rest are from his eight years of service. There are three reasons for this enormous increase: one was the increasing number of Jesuits, but more important were the aid Polanco gave Loyola in drafting letters and his organizational ability, which meant that Loyola's letters were better catalogued and preserved during those years. Letters of spiritual advice to women make up a notable part of Loyola's early correspondence, but during his last decade letters to Jesuit superiors, princes, and high churchmen predominate. Many are bland business letters, but many others are rich in spiritual advice. Usually Loyola would discuss a problem with Polanco, then have him write up a response. Loyola would make corrections, often minute, before sending out a letter. The better the style in a letter, the more quotations from classical authors or Church Fathers, the greater role Polanco probably played in its composition. Polanco also made major contributions to the Jesuit Constitutions.

Any large organization, especially a new one, needs friends in high places. This was especially true of the Jesuits, who had no financial resources of their own. For Catholic organizations good relations with the popes were obviously important. Loyola enjoyed the support of the first three popes during his Roman years. His stormy relations with Paul IV (Gianpietro Carafa) will be examined later.

Paul III (1534–1549), who was pope when Ignatius and his companions arrived in Italy, has been compared to the Roman god Janus. The month of January is named after Janus, who is usually depicted as having two faces, one looking forward, one looking back. Paul III was both the last of the Renaissance popes and the first pope of the Catholic Reformation. He was deeply involved in European politics, gave his relatives important church offices and made his Farnese family the hereditary rulers of Parma, and was a generous patron of the arts, commissioning Michelangelo's *Last Judgment* in the Sistine Chapel. But he also reacted far more vigorously than his predecessors to the challenge of Protestantism. Shortly after his election he named a group of reform-minded churchmen as cardinals and appointed them to a committee studying ways to reform the Catholic Church. Their leader was Gasparo Contarini, the supporter of the Jesuits whom we encountered earlier. After Contarini's efforts in the Regensburg Colloquy to reach a theological agreement with Lutheran theologians broke down in 1542, Paul III took a harder line and set up the Roman Inquisition to deal with heresy in much of Italy. Paul III also convoked the Council of Trent that year, but hostility between the key Catholic monarchs, Charles V and Francis I, prevented the council from opening until December 1545. Charles V wanted the council to deal first with practical reforms in the church; Paul III wanted it to start by formulating a clear Roman Catholic position on the major doctrinal issues raised by Luther and Calvin. The result was a compromise: the bishops at the council voted to devote alternating sessions to reform measures and to doctrinal issues. Since the Catholic Church would not hold another ecumenical council for the next three centuries, the decisions reached at Trent had enormous influence on Catholic teaching and practice well into the twentieth century. Laínez and Salmerón served as papal theologians during the early sessions. Paul III's appointment of members of the new religious order to such important roles was a striking vote of confidence and enhanced Jesuit prestige among bishops and rulers.

As has been seen, it was Paul III who officially approved the Society of Jesus in 1540 as a religious order. Ignatius make frequent visits to the Vatican and even a few to the papal villa at Frascati to request favors from Paul

III. Between 1541 and 1543 Loyola won many papal grants: for instance, the Jesuits were given possession of the Church of Sancta Maria della Strada and later of three small nearby churches in Rome. Three papal bulls were issued in favor of Jewish converts, and other bulls granted help for poor people and setting up a residence for former prostitutes. In 1542 Loyola helped mediate a controversy between the pope and the Portuguese king. In July 1548 Paul III issued a letter approving and praising *The Spiritual Exercises,* which was being prepared for publication—papal praise of specific books is very rare and went far toward silencing objections raised previously against the *Exercises.* Three weeks before his death Paul III extended to the Jesuits the privileges that popes had granted to the older, established religious orders.

Julius III (1550–1555) was elected only after ten bitter weeks of quarreling between the French and the Spanish factions among the cardinals. Julius leaned toward France and hence alienated Charles V. He was trained in church law but was not very pious. Given to banquets and hunting, he immediately enriched several relatives at the expense of the church. He was a generous patron of Michelangelo and of Giovanni da Palestrina, the greatest composer of Renaissance church music. Under pressure from Charles V, Julius summoned the Council of Trent back into session, but the French refused to participate, and in 1552 the French under Henry II allied with the German Lutherans and launched a war that forced the council to shut down. Julius III proved a good friend to the Jesuits. He reconfirmed their standing as a religious order and provided funding for the German College in Rome, where Jesuits supervised young Germans in training for the priesthood. Julius also supported Jesuit mission work in Asia and the Americas.

The next pope, Marcellus II, was clearly Loyola's favorite among the four popes he had contact with. Trained

Loyola meets with Pope Julius III, with whom he enjoyed cordial relations.

as a humanist, Marcellus translated Greek and Latin works into Italian; as a bishop he had promoted reforms in his diocese. Under Paul III he served as papal legate at the Council of Trent. Immediately after his election as pope he cut sharply the cost of the papal court and forbade his relatives even to come to Rome. Here at last was a pious, learned pope eager to reform the Catholic

Church. Loyola had every reason to expect excellent relations with the new pope. As a cardinal he had taken Laínez for his confessor, and had expressed great respect for Ignatius, and when Ignatius went to congratulate the new pope on his election, Marcellus promised to make good use of the Jesuits. He asked for two Jesuits to live at the papal palace and serve as his advisors. Loyola assigned Laínez and Nadal. Alas, worn out by his efforts, Marcellus suffered a fatal stroke less than three weeks after his election. Loyola later used to refer to him as "the good Pope Marcellus."

The Jesuits needed the help of secular rulers no less than that of popes. Without their support, it was hard if not impossible for the Jesuits to become established in a country. Even when rulers did not themselves directly contribute to Jesuit colleges, they could influence town governments to establish them and could often earmark funds from decayed monasteries to their support. The most powerful ruling dynasty in Europe was the Habsburgs, who were kings of Spain and emperors in Germany. They also controlled Naples, Sicily, and Milan and had reduced most of the other Italian states to satellites. Both Emperor Charles V (1519–1556) and his son Philip II (1556–1598) were staunch Catholics. Philip did not officially become king of Spain till 1556, the year of Loyola's death, but Charles made his son regent of Spain in 1543. Loyola tried to cultivate the support of both men, but they remained lukewarm toward the Jesuits. Charles's brother Ferdinand was king of Bohemia and Hungary and effective ruler in his brother's name of the Habsburg crown lands in Germany, especially Austria. Ferdinand strongly supported the Jesuits in Germany, especially Peter Canisius. The Jesuits needed his support, and he needed theirs, given the decay of the Catholic Church in the empire. Ferdinand saw the need for an effective Catholic catechism and pressured Canisius to write his catechisms and then made them mandatory throughout his realms. In 1551 he provided funding for the Jesuit college at Vienna; later that year he sent a supply of clothing to the Jesuits and brought his whole entourage to inspect the college. He promised the superior that, if the Jesuits needed anything, they should alert him because he wanted to be their protector. Chapter 15 will examine a letter Loyola sent Ferdinand on how to deal with his Protestant subjects.

The most enthusiastic patron of the Jesuits in Germany was the staunch Catholic Duke William IV of Bavaria (1508–1550), who made use of several Jesuits to shore up Catholicism at his University of Ingolstadt. His son Albert IV (1550–1579) did not continue his warm support for the Jesuits. The Jesuits often experienced such abrupt changes in princely support.

Among Europe's kings none helped the Jesuits so much as John III of Portugal (1521–1557). In August 1539 the king sent a letter to his ambassador in Rome in which he stressed the need for good priests to be sent to India and other Portuguese bases in Asia. His initiative led to Simon Rodrigues and Francis Xavier being sent to Portugal, where Rodrigues stayed and Xavier went on to India. King John provided steady support for Xavier's work.

At Lisbon Rodrigues quickly won favor at the royal court as preacher, confessor, and tutor to the crown prince. John III paid for a large residence and college for training young Jesuits at Coimbra, the seat of Portugal's leading university. By 1544 the Jesuit community numbered 45 and rose to 140 in 1551, with their living expenses being covered by the king. No other Jesuit community except the Roman College was nearly so large. At this same time many other Jesuit communities were struggling to find enough food, and Ignatius himself feared that a lawsuit might be started against the Jesuits for defaulting on a loan.

For young men of the Portuguese upper classes, joining the Jesuits became the fashionable thing to do. Portugal became the first and largest Jesuit province. Rodrigues served as its provincial superior, but his activities at court so consumed his time and energy that he neglected his work as provincial with disastrous consequences. At Coimbra there were few older Jesuits to serve as teachers and role models for the young recruits. The result was a province and a community that bordered on anarchy and created the most severe internal crisis during Loyola's years as general. He tried to call Rodrigues to Rome in 1545, but King John refused to let him go. In 1548 and again in 1553 Ignatius wrote famous letters on the Jesuit understanding of religious obedience, but many Portuguese Jesuits, including Rodrigues himself, paid little attention.

The young Jesuits at Coimbra largely broke into two very different factions. One group leaned to extreme austerities. Polanco, Loyola's secretary, described how in 1552 as a sign of repentance more than sixty young Jesuits led by their superior processed from their residence to a local church scourging themselves with whips while other Jesuits chanted hymns. The scene drew a huge crowd. Polanco commented that many spectators approved of the spectacle but many did not. On the opposite extreme, many Coimbra Jesuits wanted sumptuous foods and proudly rejected the right of superiors to give them orders.

Both extremes alarmed Ignatius. In 1552 he decided that reform must start at the top by replacing Rodrigues as provincial superior, so he wrote to the king and queen to secure their consent. He also wrote a kindly letter to Rodrigues, offering him an opportunity to serve as a missionary in Brazil (Rodrigues had once showed interest in this work) or as provincial superior in Aragon. Instead Rodrigues retired to a small Portuguese town, claiming his health was bad. Loyola appointed the Spaniard Diego

Miró, who had begun reforms as superior at Coimbra, as the new Portuguese provincial. A large number of Jesuits at Coimbra were dismissed from the order; bitter, they spread hostile insinuations. Miró quickly lost the confidence of the community at Coimbra; he got into theological disputations that were beyond his capacity, he was forgetful, his sermons were disorganized, and he had little skill in dealing with laypeople. As a result of all these troubles, roughly half the Jesuits in Portugal either left the order or were dismissed. Rodrigues himself was now ordered to leave Portugal and take over the Province of Aragon. When he argued that his bad health prevented his leaving Portugal, he was confronted with a letter from John III ordering him to go. He then went to Spain but later repeatedly evaded or disobeyed orders from Loyola to report to Rome. Had he not been one of Loyola's original companions, he almost surely would have been expelled. Loyola bent over backwards for his old friend and finally brought him round. He put in twenty years of good work in Italy and Spain before returning as an old man to Portugal.

The whole episode soured John III's attitude toward the Jesuits, who now had difficulty getting funding for necessities from the king. Doors at both the royal palace and noble households were now often closed, and even doctors did not want to see Jesuit patients. The exception was the queen, who promised her support. Some of the former Jesuits continued to preach, hear confessions, and teach catechism and claimed they were the authentic Jesuits. Rumors were spread that the archbishop of Lisbon had forbade Jesuits to preach or administer the sacraments, that Loyola was scheming to smuggle money out of Portugal, and that Rodrigues had been deposed for blocking his scheme. Many laypeople were simply befuddled by these claims. John III wrote Loyola that, if he tried to take money from the kingdom, he would stop giving the Jesuits alms. Some Jesuits saw an advantage in the whole disaster: henceforward they would trust in God and not in the favor of princes.

In Italy the most important supporters of the Jesuits were Juan de Vega and his wife, Leonor Osorio. Juan had come to know Ignatius well when he was serving as Charles V's ambassador to Rome. Later Charles appointed him viceroy of Sicily, where his help was crucial in setting up several colleges for lay students. Cosimo I, the duke of Tuscany, and his wife were generally favorable to the Jesuits but blew hot and cold about financing Jesuit colleges. They could be very insistent about requiring Jesuits, especially Diego Laínez, to preach at Florence. More helpful was Duke Ercole II d'Este of Ferrara and Modena (1534–1559), largely because his territory seemed menaced by Calvinist preachers. His wife, Renée of France, had become a Calvinist; Calvin himself visited her in 1536 and the two corresponded regularly. Modena had more Protestants than any Italian city except Lucca. Duke Ercole saw in the Jesuits a powerful counter to the Protestant preachers at Modena. Many Venetian noblemen distrusted the Jesuits because of their close ties to the papacy, so the Venetian government gave the Jesuits little support. Their main benefactor at Venice was Andrea Lippomano, who had earlier befriended Loyola. Lippomano was the administrator of a priory in Padua—in fact it was a lucrative benefice held by his family. In 1545 he turned the priorate over to Paul III, who then handed it on to the Jesuits. They used its income to set up a college at Padua where young Jesuits could live while attending lectures at the famous university. Lippomano's noble relatives resisted his alienating the priory, and after a long legal suit the case was eventually decided in the Jesuits favor in the Venetian Senate by a surprising vote of 157 to 2.

XI

The Rhythm
of Life in Rome

Loyola's working hours during his years at Rome were largely devoted to cultivating benefactors and dealing with problems arising in Jesuit communities and ministries around the world. The previous chapter examined the most important benefactors and the Portuguese crisis, the most severe internal problem during Loyola's years as general. Loyola's enormous correspondence shows how he dealt with dozens of other problems and hundreds of people. The knight of God who wanted to devote his life to working for souls in Jerusalem now had to sit at his desk writing memos or dictating letters to secretaries, much like the head of a modern corporation. He himself much preferred to work directly with people, but the greater good demanded the humdrum tasks of an administrator. Running through his correspondence and the Jesuit Constitutions is the phrase "to the greater glory of God"—*ad majorem Dei gloriam* in Latin. For centuries its abbreviation, *A.M.D.G.*, was carved on the facades of many Jesuit colleges and churches and written at the top of letters. It was the controlling principle of Loyola's life and meant that he did not have so much to abandon his romantic dreams of serving God as to adapt them to more effective ways, however prosaic. Before making a decision he tried to gather all pertinent information and consult with knowledgeable people; he then spent a good deal of time praying over the matter and seeking God's guidance. Once he had reached a decision, he tended to stick to it with great tenacity.

Like families, religious communities need buildings to live in. During their first years in Rome Ignatius and his companions shifted from building to building. Late in 1537 they took up residence in a house near the church of Trinità dei Monti as guests of its owner, the Roman gentleman Quirino Garzoni. The next year they moved twice, first to a house near the center of the city where they lived seven months, then to a building (the haunted house) belonging to Antonio Frangipani, which they rented for almost four years. In April 1541, thanks to Paul III, the Jesuits took over the Church of Santa Maria della Strada, which stood a few hundred yards east of the Palazzo Venezia, from whose balcony Mussolini harangued Fascist crowds in the 1930s. At the end of 1543 the Jesuits began building a house of their own next to the church. The following September Ignatius and the Jesuits moved into the new building, which was called the Professed House. It was remodeled and greatly expanded in 1602 and remained the headquarters of the Jesuit Order for almost three centuries. The rooms of Ignatius were preserved in the new building. Recently they have been restored to their original simplicity and are open to tourists.

Loyola's own quarters were four small rooms with low ceilings: a workroom, a bedroom, a chapel, and another bedroom for the lay brother who was his personal assistant. Two men who visited his bedroom wrote how much they were struck by how plain and neat it was. It contained only three books: the New Testament, *The Imita-*

tion of Christ by Thomas à Kempis, and a missal for celebrating mass.

Ignatius used to arise shortly after five and dress. Then he would spend perhaps half an hour in prayer before celebrating mass in the nearby chapel. As will be seen in the discussion of his spiritual diary, his mass was the high point of his day and was usually marked by his strong emotions and tears of devotion. After mass he usually spent two hours in prayer in the little chapel. He gave orders that he was not to be disturbed during this time. Repeatedly throughout the day he would take a few minutes to perform an examination of conscience—a method for reflecting on how well he was serving God. Since breakfast was not then a regular meal, the main meal came early, about ten in the morning. Supper was at six. Some days Loyola had to visit important people in various parts of the city, but most days his sole exercise was a short walk on his bad leg in a garden acquired in 1545 that was next to the Professed House. His doctor wanted him to get more exercise than he did. Most days he spent hours discussing with Polanco the right responses to his incoming mail from Jesuits and in dictating letters, then correcting them meticulously before sending out the final drafts. He also spent time writing the Jesuit Constitutions when health and correspondence gave him an opportunity.

In the evenings he would reflect on what he had done that day and what lay ahead for the next day and would make entries in his spiritual diary. Often he would step out on a small balcony and gaze at the stars; the vastness of the universe would fill him with awe at the work of the Creator. Diego Laínez described how he would stand there, take off his hat, and fix his eyes on the sky; after sinking to his knees, he would sit on a bench without noise or movement as the tears ran down his cheeks. Central to the spiritual vision he tried to inculcate in the Spiritual Exercises and in the Jesuit Constitutions was the need to find God in all things. His spiritual diary indicates that, while he walked the streets to business appointments, his mind turned to God like that hand of a compass turning north. For him there was no opposition between contemplation and action, between prayer and work. Contemplation and action fed on each other. Among the fine arts, music held the most attraction for him, going back to his days as a courtier at Arévalo; late in life at Rome he found both instrumental and choir music spiritually uplifting.

In dealing with leading churchmen in Rome, Ignatius employed the fine manners he had learned as a courtier in Spain. When he met with young Jesuits in the Roman community, he was very affable, but he could be businesslike, even gruff, in dealing with his closest associates, such as Nadal and Polanco. Loyola's first biographer was Pedro de Ribadeneira, who as a novice had lived with him in Rome; he noted that Ignatius gave milk to those who were still children in virtue, bread with crust to those making progress, but treated advance souls with rigor so that they might race toward spiritual perfection. Doubtless he felt that they were spiritually mature so that polished manners were not needed. He was very reticent about his own personal religious experiences. Sometimes when there was special need he could be very outgoing. For instance, when he was a student at Paris, he visited a friend who was both ill and extremely depressed. The friend needed cheering up and asked Ignatius to sing and dance to a Spanish jig. Ignatius did so; by putting aside his usual dignity, he succeeded in lifting his friend from depression.

In governing the Society of Jesus Ignatius could be both kindly and demanding, depending on how A.M.D.G. came into play. When admitting young men into the society, he was looking for both religious commitment and natural talent. He wanted men who were intelligent, hardworking, and mature. Good health was important because many tasks of Jesuit life required it. A good appearance too was an asset. Less important but useful was noble birth and good manners because Jesuits would often be dealing with noblemen and -women. But Ignatius always gave more weight to sound morality than to natural talent. In the first years of the society, when candidates were few, he was less demanding, but as young men began crowding in and stretching the ability of the Jesuits to feed and train them, he became more stringent. Yet he never let financial considerations block the entrance of solid candidates. He was convinced that, since God had called them, God would find a way to provide for them.

All members of his community in Rome regarded him as a father, and he tried to avoid playing favorites except for men who were ill. He kept close track of the sick and of any special food they might need. For the sick, no expense was too great. Once he sold off many of the community's dishes to buy needed medicines. Often he took personal care of the sick, acting as if he had nothing else to do. He also appreciated the need young men had for recreation, so at a time when money was very scarce, he somehow scraped together funds enough to buy a vineyard just outside Rome. There he had a small house built so that the young Jesuits studying at the Roman College could get out of the big city and relax for a day or two. He treated men who were spiritually weak gently as long there was hope for their improvement. He went out of his way to greet warmly new men who had just joined the Roman community. Often he would invite men he had to deal with to join him for a meal in his own quarters. He allowed the loquacious to ramble on without interruption, although he himself tried to be concise and clear when talking business.

In assigning men to various jobs Loyola was careful to take into consideration their talents and limitations. Before sending out the men trained at Rome, he tried to give them a test run at their future work. If someone seemed unfit for a certain job, Loyola tried to steer him away from it or removed him from it after it became clear he was unsuited. He tried to give provincial superiors freedom to execute his general directives as local circumstances and available manpower suggested. He told them to give the same freedom to local superiors.

In earlier religious orders, novices (new members) spent one year among members before taking vows. The Jesuits usually required two years. Then young men would take simple but perpetual vows binding them to the order for life. In church law, however, simple vows were easily rescinded. Loyola wanted these new Jesuits to take that lifetime commitment seriously. Understandably, some of those admitted did not measure up to Loyola's standards, and some came to realize that God had not really called them to be Jesuits. If Ignatius heard some were wavering, he prayed for them and asked them to spend some time in prayer before making any decision. If they persisted in their doubts, he gave them permission to leave the Jesuits. Those who did not measure up were encouraged to leave, and most did so after reflection. Some had to be dismissed outright, usually for failures in obedience or chastity. The Portuguese crisis was exceptional, but the dropout rate among the early Jesuits seems to have been higher than among the older religious orders.

The most famous man whom Loyola forced to leave the Jesuits was Guillaume Postel (1510–1581), a renowned linguist who had traveled in the Middle East and was eager to convert Islamic countries to Christianity. He entered the Jesuit novitiate at Rome in 1544, but his apocalyptic concerns about the end of the world alarmed Loyola, who respected Postel's learning but was deeply suspicious of his predictions. He forced Postel to leave the Jesuits the next year. Later Postel became more radical, claiming that he himself would be the firstborn of a newly restored world.

Houses of many other religious orders had a few prison cells for delinquent members. When asked whether Jesuit houses had any cells, Loyola indicated that those meriting such punishment were expelled from the Society. He was also very reluctant to allow men who had previously belonged in other religious orders to enter the Jesuits.

During his last sixteen years Ignatius remained in Rome except for four short visits to nearby towns; his days were filled with administrative duties and writing the Jesuit Constitutions. His career before settling in Rome has been called the pilgrim years, largely because they involved constant travel and because Loyola called himself "the pilgrim" in his autobiography, which stops shortly after his arrival in Rome. Loyola's pilgrim years are well suited to a narrative account that follows step-by-step the pilgrim's spiritual progress and his journeys from country to country. Although most people find his early years more interesting, they have little historical importance. Had Loyola died before settling in Rome, he would be entirely forgotten. The phrase that best describes Loyola's Roman years is *the mystic as bureaucrat*. Most readers will find that a paradox. The real inner Ignatius was the mystic, but his working hours were filled with administrative duties. The most important document revealing the central role of mystical experience in his last sixteen years consists of fragments of his spiritual diary, which we will examine in Chapter 16. They reveal that the real Ignatius was immersed in prayer and that the mystical experiences of Manresa had returned. During his years as a student he had deliberately curtailed his hours of prayer so that he could devote more time and attention to his studies. At Rome the time he devoted to prayer increased even though most of his waking hours were filled with writing or dictating the nearly 7,000 letters, memos, and directives that have come to us. He can be compared to the chief executive officers of today's multinational corporations. As general of the Company, or Society, of Jesus he had to give advice and orders to men scattered not only through much of Europe, but also Asia, Africa, and South America. He did not have the advantage of telephones or email, and it often took several years for letters from missionaries to reach Loyola in Rome and his replies to return to them.

Jesuit priests stressed active ministry to people far more than did Benedictine monks or even the medieval orders of friars, such as the Franciscans and Dominicans. Initially, the Jesuits devoted themselves to preaching, teaching catechism, and hearing confessions. Gradually education and missionary work outside Europe grew in importance. In his first years in Rome Ignatius preached frequently. His sincerity and earnestness moved his listeners far more than any formal eloquence. He tried to find time from his administrative duties to personally help people in need, and Rome was swarming with people needing spiritual and physical help. Loyola had a gift not only for personal counseling but for finding practical solutions to complex problems. Moreover, not only did he need to set a personal example for his followers, but giving direct help to people in need provided him with consolation and a break from the paperwork that consumed most of his day.

One contemporary problem was the prostitutes who walked the streets of Rome and most cities of early modern Europe. Prostitution has been called the world's oldest profession. All Christians, whether Catholic, Orthodox, or Protestant, accepted the Biblical teaching that the only proper practice of sex is in marriage. Putting that teaching into practice was no easier in Renaissance Rome than modern America. Complicating the situation during the Renaissance was the fact that males from the upper classes tended to postpone marriage till their late twenties or even longer. Women usually married in their late teens. During the years when their sex drives were strongest, many young males turned to prostitutes. Most cities either regulated brothels or looked the other way from freelance prostitution. People justified this policy by citing the opinion of Saint Augustine that tolerating prostitution was a lesser evil than having randy young men rape respectable women. Poverty pressured many young women into prostitution, which at times could be lucrative but also carried a badge of shame that later hindered former prostitutes from finding husbands. Many cities in Italy and Spain had convents for ex-prostitutes. These nuns were called the *conversae*, the converted.

In 1543 Rome had a convent that sheltered eighty of these women, but many ex-prostitutes had previously been married and thus had to explore the possibility of returning to their husbands. Others needed time to decide whether they wanted to become nuns or to seek a husband. In January 1543 Loyola stepped in and opened the House of Saint Martha, a halfway house where ex-prostitutes could live while they sorted out what they wanted to do with the rest of their lives. Between 1543 and 1550 some three hundred women stayed at the House of Saint Martha in transition to marriage and respectability. Ignatius had also befriended several wealthy women in Rome, for instance Margaret of Austria, the illegitimate daughter of Emperor Charles V. On Loyola's recommendation wealthy women accepted ex-prostitutes into their household staffs. Notable among them was Vittoria Colonna, the greatest woman poet of the century. Saint Martha's needed financing; here again Loyola was fortunate. Some ancient statues were discovered while the foundation was being dug for a new Jesuit residence in Rome. Ignatius sold the statues to connoisseurs and directed that the money be used to endow Saint Martha's. He also enlisted wealthy benefactors for this cause.

To cover the ongoing expenses of Saint Martha's, he turned to a contemporary institution, the confraternity, and established the Company of Grace, which Paul III approved in 1543. In the late Middle Ages and even more in early modern Europe down to the French Revolution, Catholic cities had many confraternities, some for men, some for women, some for both. Many people belonged to several confraternities, which combined social activism, mutual friendship, and religious devotion. Most confraternities had a chapel, sometimes even a whole church, where the members would gather for prayer or liturgical services. Members might then convene for a banquet. Confraternities often marched in funeral processions for dead colleagues, and some provided members with dowries for their daughters. Loyola's Company of Grace included many of the leading women of Rome as well as fourteen cardinals. In this way the upkeep of St. Martha's was covered.

"An ounce of prevention is worth a pound of cure," goes the old saw. Many single young women resorted to prostitution because of poverty. Many prostitutes pressured their own daughters into that "profession," or at least gave them a bad example. In April 1546 Loyola set up the Hospice of Saint Catherine near Rome's first Jesuit church. In this hospice girls aged ten to twelve could avoid such pressures. Once again, he started a confraternity, the Company of Unfortunate Young Women, to support the hospice. He also helped in raising funds for a boys' orphanage that Cardinal Gianpietro Carafa had established earlier.

Inflation and other factors forced many of the lower nobility in Rome into poverty, similar to the situation in Barcelona noted earlier. Their noble status made public begging socially unacceptable. Many cities set up special arrangements so that they could receive alms without having to beg in public. Ignatius founded the Company of the Twelve Apostles, a confraternity to assist impoverished noblemen. When such men came to his door seeking help, he gave them minor tasks and had them paid very generously so that technically they were not begging.

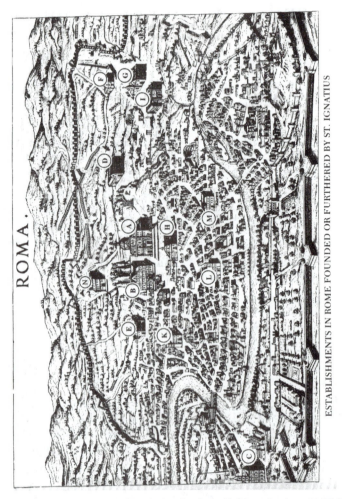

ESTABLISHMENTS IN ROME FOUNDED OR FURTHERED BY ST. IGNATIUS

Establishments in Rome founded or furthered by Ignatius Loyola. This illustration is reproduced with the permission of the Institute of Jesuit Sources from p. 576 of William Bangert, *The History of the Society of Jesus* (St. Louis: Institute of Jesuit Sources, 1986). A. The Gesù church where Loyola is buried. B. The Roman College. C. Residence for Jesuit priests working at St. Peter's Basilica. D. House for Jesuit novices. E. and F. Orphanages for boys and girls that Loyola helped. G. House for Jews preparing for baptism. H. Saint Martha's house for converted prostitutes. I. Saint Catherine's home for young women to help them avoid prostitution. K. The German College. L. The English College, founded shortly after Loyola's death. M. Roman Seminary, to train priests. N. Maronite Seminary, to train priests from the Middle East.

Loyola's work for needy people in Rome illustrates not just a warm heart but his remarkable ability to find practical solutions and to enlist and organize the elite in meeting the long-term needs of the poor. He accomplished this despite being a Spaniard who never learned to speak Italian well and did it at a time when most Romans harbored bitter memories of Spanish soldiers sacking Rome in 1527.

Loyola's actions for the spiritual care of dying people would earn little sympathy today. Medieval church legislation required doctors to stop helping patients who refused to receive the last sacraments. Increasingly doctors ignored this legislation. They did not want to alarm patients by urging them to receive the last sacraments, so they often postponed calling for a priest until a patient was no longer mentally competent. Loyola believed that patients' eternal salvation was more important than their psychological comfort. He argued that if a patient refused the sacraments three times, the doctor should refuse further medical help. His proposal was accepted by two groups of theologians who discussed it before bringing it to Pope Paul III, who ordered that Loyola's proposal be put into practice in Rome, although not throughout the papal states.

Rome had a considerable Jewish community. The popes had been far more tolerant toward Jews than most other Christian rulers. Jews were expelled from England in 1290 and from France in 1306. As has been seen, in 1492 Spanish Jews were ordered to convert to Catholicism or leave Spain. Many old Christians in Spain resented the success of converted Jews and doubted the sincerity of their faith. Partly under royal pressure, the religious orders in Spain refused to accept new members of Jewish ancestry. Loyola did not share that attitude; indeed, he openly stated that he regretted not belonging to the same race as Jesus and resisted the Spanish government when it tried to prevent the Jesuits from accepting men of Jewish ancestry. Diego Laínez, the second superior general of the Jesuits, was of

Jewish descent. So too was Juan Polanco, Loyola's secretary, and Francisco de Toledo, the first Jesuit cardinal. Leon Poliakoff, the great historian of anti-Semitism, claims, "The only man who was able in his lifetime to ignore the taboo of *Limpieza* [purity of blood] was Ignacio de Loyola. High birth as well as missionary genius made the founder of the Jesuit order immune to this racist contagion." Loyola was eager to convert as many Roman Jews as possible. Here he again managed to get Paul III to abrogate the practice that, if a Jew converted, his wealth would be confiscated and his children had no claims on it. Obviously this discouraged Jews from accepting baptism. To make conversion easier Loyola set up two houses, one for men, the other for women, where Jewish converts could stay while they made the transition to their new faith, without having to live with Jewish parents. He obtained papal approval for this project and secured financial help from Margaret of Austria and from the duchess of Castro, who was related to the papal family.

XII

Loyola, the Jesuits, and Education

Loyola and his early companions planned to devote themselves to preaching, administering communion and confession, serving as missionaries, and teaching children catechism. They did not plan to get into education or running schools, yet by Loyola's death the Jesuits were operating thirty schools, and more Jesuits were engaged in teaching than in any other work. Loyola originally expected most Jesuit priests to live in and minister from what he called Professed Houses, that is, communities where preachers and confessors could live together as a community while working in nearby churches. The Professed Houses were to have no fixed income but were to depend on gifts from the people. There were only two of these by 1556. Gradually it became clear to Loyola that the Professed Houses were rarely financially viable, while schools were both needed and popular. Loyola was both a religious dreamer and an adaptable pragmatist who saw God's hand in what worked. Schools quickly replaced Professed Houses as the main Jesuit ministry.

The first Jesuits who became teachers did so because of immediate needs. In 1537, just after Ignatius and his companions arrived in Rome, Paul III asked Laínez and Faber to teach at the University of Rome. In Germany there was an acute shortage of Catholic theologians, so Peter Faber taught during 1542–1543 at the University of Mainz, and the next year Claude Jay did the same at the University of Ingolstadt in Bavaria. In 1549 Duke William IV of Bavaria obtained the services of Jay, Alfonso Salmerón, and Peter Canisius to teach theology at Ingolstadt. Canisius, known as the pioneer Jesuit of Germany, later served as dean, rector, and vice chancellor of the university. Still, these were all individual assignments and contributed little to later models of Jesuit education.

When Francis Xavier arrived in Goa in 1542, the main Portuguese base in India, he found a small school called the College of Saint Paul for non-Portuguese boys that a local confraternity had established in the hope that some of its graduates would become priests. Most of its sixty students were Indians, but there was a sprinkling of Malays and Africans. The Africans were mainly sons of slaves. The governor of Goa and other local leaders tried to enlist Xavier's help. Xavier had no men to spare as teachers but wrote a glowing letter to Loyola about the prospects of the college, which he felt would soon have six hundred students. In this he was overly optimistic, but as more Jesuits arrived from Europe, a number of them were assigned to teach and administer the college.

The remote college at Goa was the first school to come under Jesuit direction, but it had little effect on Jesuit education in Europe, where Jesuit involvement began slowly. While many of the early recruits to the Jesuits were mature men and already university trained, increasingly they were young men in their late teens or early twenties who needed more education, especially in philosophy and theology, if they were to become priests. To train these younger Jesuits, Loyola set up Jesuit communities near established universities, notably in Paris, Rome, Padua, Coimbra, and

Louvain in Belgium. These communities were called colleges, but initially they were merely residences for Jesuit students who attended lectures at the nearby universities. Later a few supplementary courses were taught in the community to young Jesuits. Still later, lay students began to attend those courses, and gradually a few Jesuit colleges independent of the nearby universities evolved.

The first Jesuit school in Europe began at the request of Francis Borgia, the duke of Gandia. In 1545 Borgia decided to set up a minicollege on his estates to train young Jesuits. The next year he used his prestige and influence to gain from the pope a university charter for his little college and persuaded Loyola to allow some lay students to attend classes. The college/university at Gandia was the first independent school with Jesuit teachers, but it was atypical of the Jesuit colleges which followed. It had only a handful of lay students, it was not near a university or a city, and its lay students were mainly the sons of Morisco peasants. Later Jesuit colleges were in cities and mainly attracted middle- and upper-class students. Any prospects of expansion at Gandia were soon wiped out when Borgia's son refused to provide the financial support his father had arranged before he resigned as duke and became a Jesuit.

The real breakthrough for Jesuit education came at Messina, in Sicily, then one of Europe's largest cities. Here the initiative was taken by the Spanish viceroy Juan de Vega and his wife, Leonor Osorio. As noted earlier, they had come to know Loyola and the Jesuits well when de Vega had served as ambassador for Charles V to the papal court. De Vega urged the Messina city officials to petition Loyola for five teachers and five Jesuit students to open a college that would teach grammar, rhetoric, the arts, and theology. With help from the viceroy the city officials promised to provide a school building, plus food, lodging, and clothing for the Jesuits. At Loyola's insistence, the early Jesuit schools charged no tuition, but this meant that adequate financing had to be provided by either private benefactors or town governments. Often the income of church benefices, such as rents owed to decayed monasteries, were earmarked for the new Jesuit colleges.

Loyola sent ten Jesuits to Messina, where the college opened early in 1548. Four of them were priests, all exceptionally talented, for Loyola wanted to get the college off to a good start. None of the four priests was an Italian—a Spaniard, a Frenchman, a Belgian, and a Dutchman. This international mix was possible because courses were taught in Latin. The six younger Jesuits, called scholastics, were initially sent to pursue their own studies, but they too gradually became involved in teaching. To win support for their schools, the Jesuits usually opened the school year with speeches and presentations by faculty and students before local dignitaries. Loyola's secretary, Juan Polanco, described the ceremonies at Messina: "The reopening of classes in October [1549] was preceded by three days of public disputations which featured all the subjects which [the Jesuits] were going to teach. This took place to the great edification of the spectators and added to the enthusiasm [of the students]. . . . The viceroy . . . was in attendance along with the judges and all the leading men of the city, and he listened to orations and poems linked to the reopening of classes." Later Jesuit schools added dramas that combined religious content and spectacle. Jesuit plays written in German-speaking lands have been studied more carefully than elsewhere; more than 7,500 plays were written there between 1553 and 1773. One author was Saint Edmund Campion (1540–1581), whose plays entertained the court of Emperor Rudolf II at Prague before Campion was sent as a missionary to England, where he was martyred.

Jerome Nadal, the Jesuit superior at Messina, sent Loyola such enthusiastic reports about the success of the Messina college that he was convinced to channel more Jesuits into education. News of the college at Messina quickly led Palermo and other cities in Sicily to ask Loyola for colleges. In the last five years of Loyola's life, the Jesuits were opening colleges at a rate of five per year. Education quickly became the main Jesuit ministry. Most of these new colleges were in Italy, but those in Spain, Portugal, France, and Germany tended to enroll more students than did the Italian colleges.

In December 1551 Ignatius had his secretary, Polanco, draft letters to the Jesuits in Spain and Portugal encouraging them to open colleges and suggested ways to line up the necessary funding from rulers and benefactors. The letter to Spain lists fifteen reasons for starting the schools. Four deal with ways the schools will help the Jesuits themselves: younger Jesuits will master what they teach, learn how to apply themselves diligently, and will gain self-confidence; moreover, some students will want to join the Jesuits. Students will learn from their studies, especially poor students who can not afford schools that charge tuition. Catechism lessons will deepen their faith and encourage virtues. The colleges will also benefit society, especially parents who are hard-pressed to pay tuition. Jesuit teachers will also do some preaching and administering of the sacraments; this will benefit the city and encourage parents to be good examples for their children. The Jesuits were also to encourage the townsfolk to support hospitals for the sick and refuge homes for former prostitutes and other charitable works. Finally, graduates will enter careers in church, government, or business and will bring to their work a sense of responsibility for others.

In that same month, Loyola had Polanco send another general letter to all Jesuits which stressed that "we accept for our classes and literary studies all boys, rich or poor, free of charge and for charity's sake without accepting remuneration." Free tuition obviously was popular with parents, but it meant that the Jesuits had to curry the favor of princes and city officials to come up with funding. Sometimes towns and princes promised financing but reneged once the school was set up. Sometimes, especially in small towns, poor funding and low enrollment forced schools to close after a few years.

The new schools were not set up without friction. Local schoolmasters were often driven out of business and forced to seek jobs in smaller towns because the Jesuit schools were usually better and always cheaper. The first Jesuit schools taught the rudiments of Latin, but as the demand for Jesuit schools outstripped the available Jesuits, Loyola decided in 1551 that students in the newer Jesuit colleges would need to know how to read and write and have some knowledge of Latin grammar before they could be admitted. In older Jesuit schools the lowest levels were to be gradually phased out. That had the advantage of leaving an opening for local schoolmasters but meant that poor parents would have to pay for their sons to learn the basics of Latin. Few could afford this, so more and more the students at Jesuit schools were sons of doctors, lawyers, merchants, and the nobility. Loyola wanted to get new schools off to a good start, so he did what he had done at Messina: he sent the best men he had available, but after a few years he pulled them out and sent in less experienced teachers, often to the annoyance of students and parents. Most Jesuit colleges had attached to them a church where Jesuit priests could preach, preside at Mass, and hear confessions.

When Loyola died in 1556, there were 34 Jesuit schools. By 1581 there were 144; by 1615 there were 372, and their number continued to rise until the Jesuits were suppressed in 1773. Jesuit colleges dominated secondary education in Catholic countries of Europe and played a major role in education from Goa, India, to Lima, Peru. The Jesuits were restored in 1814 but grew more slowly; once more education was their main ministry, especially in the United States, where today there are twenty-one Jesuit universities, plus colleges and high schools.

What did the Jesuits teach in their schools? Jesuit schools of the Renaissance were called colleges, but these colleges were roughly equivalent to junior high school through junior college in America today. Enrollment at their schools fell off sharply as students entered their late teens and either went on to the traditional universities or went to work, often depending on whether their parents could afford their further education. Only a few Jesuit schools offered university degrees. Here the pioneer college at Messina was typical. In its first full year it had 180 students in the beginning class of Latin grammar; this was soon split into three grammar classes of ascending difficulty. Students did not pass from one level to the next according to a fixed calendar but rather moved up, usually as a group but sometimes as individuals, after they had proved their mastery of the material on the lower level. This could take place anytime during the academic year. After grammar came the humanities and then rhetoric. In these more advanced classes they read extensively in Cicero and the classical Latin writers prized by Renaissance humanists. For any student thinking about attending a university, mastery of Latin was absolutely necessary because lectures, examinations, and textbooks in all the universities of Europe were in Latin. After students had mastered Latin grammar they were introduced to Greek grammar and gradually to Greek authors of increasing difficulty. Higher-level classes included logic, philosophy, and scholastic theology, plus some mathematics and Hebrew, but enrollment in advanced classes was low at most Jesuit schools during Loyola's lifetime.

Students were expected to attend Mass daily and go to confession once a month, but classes in catechism were restricted to one class per week plus holidays. Still, religion permeated the atmosphere of the colleges, and the strict

Major Jesuit communities, 1540–1556.

discipline cut down on rowdy behavior, swearing, and cheating, and inculcated temperance and obedience to parents. Needless to say, the Latin and Greek writings covered in the classroom stressed authors who taught good morality. Thus the bawdier plays of Aristophanes, Plautus, and Terence were avoided, while literature courses concentrated on the sanitized and uplifting works of writers such as Cicero, Seneca, and Plato. No Greek author was more central than Aristotle; his philosophical and scientific teachings dominated both Protestant and Catholic schools until the mid-seventeenth century. As noted earlier, Loyola chose Thomas Aquinas as the official theologian of the Jesuit order. His choice was influenced by the training that Loyola and his first companions had received in Paris, where courses in philosophy and theology rested largely on Aristotle and Aquinas.

As the Jesuit schools grew, they began offering more advanced courses in philosophy and theology; these were subjects that had been the preserve of universities. The result was tension in university towns. University professors and administrators complained to civil authorities that the Jesuit schools were creeping into higher education, where the university had a legal monopoly. They were also drawing students away from the universities, not least because they charged no tuition. Sometimes the tension was ideological. Thus professors in Paris believed that the Jesuit loyalty to the papacy might endanger the traditional liberties claimed by the Catholic church in France. In Paris in 1565 the university and its supporters brought eight lawsuits against the Jesuits, and university students smashed the windows of the Jesuit college and dumped in manure. The students of the Jesuit college retaliated in kind. In Venice local teachers encouraged similar demonstrations against the new Jesuit college. In Padua the Jesuits in their classes attacked philosophy professors at the university for denying that reason could prove the immortality of the soul. The professors in turn attacked the Jesuits for the use of superficial textbooks in philosophy. The university professors in their lectures had to explain difficult passages in texts of Aristotle line by line, while the Jesuit textbooks glided over these problems. The Jesuits usually lost their fights with the universities; their colleges were closed down in Padua in 1591 and in Paris and Louvain in 1595, the sites of Europe's three leading Catholic universities. The controversy in Padua climaxed when university students invaded classrooms in the Jesuit college, stripped off their clothing, shouted obscenities at the teachers, and then paraded naked back to their lodgings.

The curriculum at Jesuit colleges was not particularly innovative. Renaissance humanists had been urging a similar curriculum for years, and the Lutheran academy at Strasbourg had implemented it more than a decade before the Jesuit college at Messina. More innovative, especially in Italy, were some of the teaching methods. Loyola increasingly urged that Jesuit colleges should have an adjacent church where students could take lessons in catechism and receive the sacraments, thus linking education to religious practice. Just noted was the use of textbooks written for students that made a systematic presentation of a course's subject matter; the explosive growth of Jesuit colleges after 1550 provided a market for such textbooks. The majority of students at Jesuit colleges ranged from age ten to sixteen, although students of philosophy and theology were older. Most Renaissance educators believed that, for young boys, sparing the rod would spoil the child. Loyola basically disagreed; physical punishment should be kept to a minimum and was never to be applied by a Jesuit. The schools hired a layman for that task.

The school term ran nearly year-round six days a week, with only a week or two in summer for vacation. The many religious holidays meant that there were about 270 school days a year, but the school day usually lasted only five hours. The beginning grammar classes were often large, fifty or more students, so that the Jesuit teachers recruited student to help with routine work. A student (called a decurion) would be put in charge of nine of his fellows. His job was to take their attendance, gather their homework, and run an oral recitation session and report the results to the teacher. Then the Jesuit teacher put the decurion himself through an oral recitation of the day's work. The position of decurion was rotated periodically. The Jesuits believed in competition to motivate students and held frequent contests in which students made written or oral presentations in Latin or Greek. Winners could earn honorable Roman titles such as *general* or *senator* until the next competition a month later. More important were special celebrations to which parents and civic officials were invited; on these occasions outstanding students gave orations or read their essays. Even more elaborate were the school dramas noted earlier. In an age before electronic media these celebrations were high points in the calendar for many towns.

The most important decision Loyola made regarding curriculum and teaching method was his insistence that Jesuit schools follow the "method and order of Paris." His own first efforts at a university education in Alcalá and Salamanca had been a failure, largely because those universities had no fixed sequence of courses. In Paris, especially at the College of Saint Barbe, he found a sequence that forced him to take basic courses first, then move forward steadily through grammar, rhetoric, poetry, literature, and history, then on to philosophy and theology. The universities of Germany and Italy, like those of Spain, allowed students to choose courses in a haphazard way, usually to their own detriment. Ignatius was determined that this would not happen in Jesuit colleges. In Paris students were also not allowed to merely sit back and listen to lectures; they were called upon to participate actively and prove their mastery of a unit in drills and repetitions. This too Loyola adopted for Jesuit schools.

Loyola adopted the Paris method in his Constitutions for the Jesuit order, Part IV, chapters 11–17, but added refinements learned from trial and error at the Jesuit schools during the last eight years of his life. It is typical of Loyola's attention to detail that, before writing this part of the Constitutions, he tried to get copies of the constitutions of nine universities so that he could comb them for ideas. As he wrote, "after seeing what other universities employ and practice, and what is fitting to our Institute and manner of proceeding, general constitutions can be composed to serve the universities and also the colleges of the Society." While the Jesuit Constitutions continued to govern Jesuit colleges, the rapid expansion of colleges after Loyola's death and growing experience in teaching forced the Jesuits to fine-tune the techniques of and regulations at their colleges. Three major efforts were made to draw up an effective plan of studies (or *ratio studiorum*). A huge third draft of a *ratio* was circulated in 1591 to Jesuit colleges but was severely criticized. In 1599 a final draft of the *Ratio Studiorum* (shorter, but still 208 pages long) was made the official guide for Jesuit schools and remained in use until the early twentieth century.

The college at Messina may have been the pioneer Jesuit college, but the most important Jesuit school founded during Loyola's lifetime was the Roman College, now known as the Gregorian University because of financial help from Pope Gregory XIII (1572–1585). The Roman College was opened in February 1551, thanks to a small endowment from Francis Borgia. Initially courses were restricted to Latin and Greek, but the curriculum included literature and philosophy by 1553. The Roman College was distinctive for several reasons. Ignatius considered Rome the center of the world and called outstanding Jesuit professors to Rome from every land. The Roman College was a full-fledged university, not primarily a secondary school like Messina and most other Jesuit colleges. Loyola himself wrote the rules for the Roman College.

Loyola encouraged Jesuit superiors to send young Jesuits to Rome to complete their education in philosophy and theology, and they responded enthusiastically. By 1555 there were Jesuit students in Rome from more than ten countries, but the college was so weak financially that during that year Ignatius had to send a hundred of them back to their home countries lest they starve. Gradually the finances improved, and five years after Loyola's death a Jesuit wrote to his successor Laínez, "I believe that one day, like the Trojan horse, [the Roman College] will launch forth [priests] to overrun and conquer the world."

Linked to the Roman College was the German College, where German students lived under the supervision of the Jesuits while taking courses at the Roman College. The German College, which also had some Czech, Hungarian, and Polish students, was set up for students studying for the diocesan priesthood. The universities back in their home countries often had Protestant professors who, it was feared, might undermine commitment of students to Catholicism. It was Cardinal Giovanni Morone, who had much experience as papal nuncio in Germany, who suggested the college to Loyola and secured the support of Pope Julius III for it. Loyola hoped that the students' years in Rome would ensure their loyalty to the papacy. After some difficult early years, the German College began to attract the sons of wealthy and noble families. They paid no tuition for courses at the Roman College but did have to pay their living expenses. Partly because of their family connections, many of the students became bishops and played a key role in the revival of German Catholicism in the late sixteenth century. In May 1554 English students began attending the German College, but later a separate English College was started. Later in 1554 Loyola agreed to the suggestion of King Ferdinand that a separate college for Hungarians similar to the German College be set up in Rome.

XIII

Loyola, the Jesuits, and Women

Between 1573 and 1575 Juan Polanco, who had served as Loyola's secretary from 1547 till Loyola's death, wrote a very detailed chronicle of Jesuit history during Loyola's lifetime—some 4,500 pages long. Repeatedly he points out that the preaching of the Jesuits was more effective among women than among men, especially in encouraging women to frequent communion and confession. Most of the earlier religious orders, such as the Benedictines and Franciscans, had both male and female branches. As the reputation of the Jesuits spread, it was almost inevitable that women would desire to join the Jesuits by setting up a female branch, just as Saint Clare had done for the Franciscans. For reasons we will explore shortly, however, Loyola and most of his companions did not want a female branch of the Jesuits.

Loyola was deeply indebted to Isabel Roser, who had generously helped him when he was studying in Barcelona after his return from the Holy Land. Loyola sent her several of his earliest letters, rich in spiritual advice. After the death of her husband in 1542, she left

Barcelona with her maid, Francisca Cruillas, and with another noble woman, Isabel de Josa. Their intention was to put themselves under obedience to Ignatius—in effect to start a branch of the Jesuits for women. He refused their offer, and de Josa returned to Spain, but an Italian woman, Lucrezia di Biadene, joined Roser and her maid. In 1545 Roser wrote to Paul III requesting permission for the three women to take vows as Jesuits and asking the pope to order Loyola to accept their vows. The pope issued a written order granting their request. Loyola had to comply. On Christmas day the three women made solemn vows of poverty, chastity, and obedience before Loyola himself in the Jesuit Church of Santa Maria della Strada. During Loyola's lifetime only 5 percent of male Jesuits were allowed to take solemn vows, partly because most of them were still in training. Where should the three women Jesuits live? Loyola sent them to the House of Saint Martha, the convent for converted prostitutes that he had set up earlier, and put a Spanish Jesuit lay brother at their disposal as a servant. Their relationship with Ignatius soon soured. Roser began to complain that the Jesuits were taking over her possessions. Her nephew came to Rome and backed up her claims so that a legal inquiry was launched. It revealed that, in fact, the contribution of the Jesuits to her support was notably larger than her gifts to them. On 30 September 1546 the quarrel was resolved with the help of Leonor Osorio, wife of the Spanish ambassador. The three women and a priest from Barcelona met with Loyola and three other Jesuits and reached an agreement. The next day Ignatius dispensed the three women from their vows, an action for which he had previously obtained the pope's permission. Roser returned to Barcelona and entered a Franciscan convent, where she died in 1554. One might expect that the whole Roman experience left her with bitter memories, but in two later letters to Loyola she expressed her gratitude to him and sorrow for the trouble she had caused.

In May 1547 Loyola wrote Paul III and requested that henceforward the Jesuit order should not have women under its obedience. The pope issued the requested mandate. But that did not end the question. Two nuns at a Barcelona convent, Teresa Rajadell and Jerónina Oluja (the convent's prioress), sought to put themselves under obedience to Loyola because their Benedictine convent was so lax. Ignatius had also known Rejadella since his days as a student in Barcelona, and she was a woman much respected for her holiness. Sixteen letters of their correspondence have survived, running from 1536, when he was in Venice, till 1552. His early letters to her are rich in spiritual advice, while their later correspondence mainly deals with the request of the two nuns to be accepted into the Jesuits. Ignatius refused their request but encouraged them to strive to reform their convent. He cited the papal directive against Jesuits taking over the governance or spiritual direction of nuns and argued that such links to a convent were incompatible with the Jesuits' calling "to hurry to any part of the world where . . . the needs of the neighbor should summon them." Loyola was also well aware that becoming involved with the controversies at the Barcelona convent would draw the Jesuits into a number of ongoing lawsuits. On her death bed in July 1553 Rajadell asked her confessor to write Ignatius and beg him "to keep a place for her convent in his heart."

But there was one last woman Jesuit, a person Ignatius could not refuse: Princess Juana of Spain. She was the daughter of Emperor Charles V and the sister of Philip II. She was only five in 1540, when Antonio de Araoz, a relative of Ignatius and the first Jesuit provincial superior in Spain, preached to the women of the royal court. Two years later her chaplain entered the Jesuits. Her connections with the Jesuits continued to multiply. Unhappily married to the young and sickly heir to the Portuguese throne, she was lonely and bored when Francis Borgia visited the Portuguese court in 1553; to relieve her boredom Borgia invented for her use a card game that carried a religious message. Her husband died on January 2, 1554, eighteen days before she gave birth to his son, the future King Sebastian of Portugal. Soon afterwards she returned to the Spanish court. When Prince Philip left for England in July to visit his new wife, Queen Mary Tudor, he appointed Juana regent, or acting ruler, of Spain. Ignatius welcomed the appointment: "I hope that His Divine majesty will employ their [the people of Spain] help in his service for the common good." In her five years' service as regent, Juana combined determination, intelligence, and a deep faith with a certain touchiness about her dignity. One Venetian ambassador reporting to his masters described her as a dazzling vision. A later Venetian ambassador noted that she was living a kind of monastic life. In fact she had become a secret Jesuit, something she did not reveal even to her brother, Philip II. Soon after she returned to Spain and took over the duties of regent, she summoned Borgia to be her spiritual advisor. He could not ignore the request of a princess-regent. Araoz also came to the court and preached before Juana. Unlike Ignatius, he favored a female branch of the Jesuits and may have encouraged her. Late in 1554 Borgia wrote Loyola that Juana had decided to become a Jesuit. Their correspondence about the princess always gave her a code name, Mateo Sánchez.

The news put Loyola in a no-win situation. He did not want responsibility for a women's order. If news that the princess was becoming a Jesuit got out, similar requests would multiply. In October Loyola gathered a meeting of key Jesuits in Rome to discuss the situation. They could not simply deny entrance to the princess. Her father, Charles V, had always been lukewarm toward the Jesuits.

A refusal might incur his wrath and perhaps that of Prince Philip. But Juana was still only nineteen and beautiful. The empire of the Habsburgs had been built on royal marriages much more than on military victories. Charles or Philip might call on her at any time to undertake another political marriage. But to refuse her request outright would anger her and might hurt the Jesuits throughout Habsburg lands. Loyola and his advisors decided on a compromise solution: they admitted the princess to the society with the same simple vows as young Jesuit scholastics, men in training for the priesthood. These vows were binding for life on the individual, but they could be easily canceled by superiors, unlike solemn vows. Henceforward Juana considered herself a Jesuit and intervened several times to protect the society from its enemies in Spain. She also donated 3,000 ducats to found a Jesuit college at Valladolid, a very considerable sum. Ignatius kept careful and grateful track of these services. She remained a Jesuit till her death in 1573.

Why did Loyola not want a female branch of the Jesuits when so many previous religious orders had had branches for women? There were several reasons. He believed that the mobility that should characterize Jesuits was incompatible with their being tied down as chaplains or confessors for nuns. The essence of Jesuit life was active service to others, but all religious communities for women up to this time had been cloistered; nuns were to remain in their convents and devote themselves to prayer. Many convents did take in and train girls of the upper classes, but that was their only active ministry.

Widespread among reform-minded churchmen of Loyola's time was the conviction that the breakdown of cloister was responsible for sinful behavior among nuns, especially regarding chastity. In 1563 the Council of Trent sought a quick fix for unchaste behavior: lock nuns in their convents and restrict their contact with the outside world. The regulations of the council did much to prevent abuses among nuns but forfeited many good works that women could contribute to the church and society. There were attempts to get around these regulations. Thus Mary Ward (1585–1646) and other nuns, known as the English Ladies and sometimes the English Jesuitesses, worked underground in England to help persecuted Catholics. In Protestant England cloistered convents were utterly impossible. Despite the success of their work, there were complaints that the English Ladies were doing works "unsuitable to their sex, capacity and their feminine modesty." A papal bull suppressed their work in 1631.

XIV

Opponents of Loyola and the Jesuits

Few organizations in history have been so greatly praised or widely condemned as the Society of Jesus, and this has been the case from Loyola's time to our own. Webster's gives two definitions for the word *Jesuit:* "a member of a religious society for men founded by St. Ignatius of Loyola" and a person "given to intrigue or equivocation." The adjective *jesuitical* is derogatory in all Western languages. As we have seen, the term *Jesuit* was coined by enemies of the Society of Jesus and only taken up later by members of the order because it was convenient and already widespread. In the eyes of Protestants and many Catholics the name the Jesuits took for themselves—Society, or Company, of Jesus—reeked of arrogance by comparison with the names of previous religious orders. Typical of sixteenth-century Protestant attitudes toward the Jesuits was Sir Walter Mildmay, a leading politician under Elizabeth I, who wrote that the pope had sent to England "a sort of hypocrites, naming themselves Jesuits, a rabble of vagrant friars newly sprung up and coming through the world to trouble the Church of God, whose principal errand is, by creeping into the houses and familiarities of men of behavior and reputation, not only to corrupt the realm with false doctrine, but also, under that pretense, to stir sedition."

The opposition to Loyola and the early Jesuits sprang from a great variety of attitudes and belief systems. Thus some opponents were Protestants, others were conservative Catholics. Some people opposed the spread of the Jesuits for financial reasons, some because of nationality conflicts, most because of religious differences. It is easy to understand, for instance, the hostility of local schoolmasters who were driven out of business by the spread of Jesuit schools.

Curiously, many of the most bitter opponents of the Jesuits were Spanish churchmen. The Catholic church since the Middle Ages has been cursed with rivalry between religious orders, for instance, between the Dominicans and the Franciscans. By the end of the sixteenth century there were bitter theological controversies between the Dominicans, who stressed the role of divine predestination, and the Jesuits, who gave a larger role to human free will in explaining how people attain salvation. But this controversy developed after Loyola's death. During his lifetime many Dominicans, including their superior general and the official theologian of the pope, were favorable to the Jesuits. But several influential Dominicans in Spain saw the Jesuits as heretics and a danger to the Catholic faith at a time when Catholicism was in retreat in most of northern Europe before the forces of Protestantism.

The most bitter and vocal critic of the Jesuits was Melchor Cano (1509–1560), perhaps the most influential Catholic theologian of his generation. He had studied at the University of Salamanca while Loyola was a student there and undoubtedly knew of his brief imprisonment by the Dominicans. Cano regarded Loyola as an *alumbrado*—a person who depended on inner light from

God and disregarded both scripture and the institutional church. He attacked the Jesuits both in sermons and lectures and denounced them to the Royal Council. Even though *The Spiritual Exercises* had the explicit approval of the pope, he regarded some of its rules as poisonous. In one of his attacks on the Jesuits he says that he had met Loyola three times in Rome, in 1542, it seems. On one occasion Ignatius invited him to dinner at the Jesuit house. The three meetings served only to convince Cano that Loyola was ignorant of both human and divine law, imprudent, pompous, and full of vainglory. Later Cano claimed that making the Spiritual Exercises turned soldiers into women and knights into hens. Less famous but no less hostile was another Dominican, Tomás Pedroche, who was commissioned by the cardinal-archbishop of Toledo to examine the *Exercises*. He too regarded Loyola as an ignorant, lazy *alumbrado* who had fled Spain and gone to Rome to avoid the Inquisition. The gifted Dominican spiritual writer Luis de Granada saw in Loyola's rules for mental prayer a modern invention likely to drive people mad.

But the most dangerous of the Spanish Dominican enemies of the Jesuits was Juan Alvarez de Silíceo, the cardinal-archbishop of Toledo and head of the Catholic church in Spain. In 1552 he refused to allow Jesuits to administer the sacraments in his jurisdiction because the society accepted men of Jewish ancestry, contrary to the practice of the other religious orders in Spain. Although Ignatius and most of his first companions were Spaniards, the early growth of the Jesuits was much slower in Spain than in Portugal and Italy. This was largely due to the opposition of leading churchmen such as Cano and Silíceo. Fortunately for the Jesuits, the prestige of Francis Borgia gradually worked to counteract that opposition.

Ignatius and his original companions took great pride in having studied at the University of Paris, so that the hostility they met from the university and its conservative faculty of theology, known as the Sorbonne, must have been especially painful to them. That hostility, which was noted earlier, would endure for centuries. During the early years of the Reformation, Catholics branded Protestants with the Latin word *novatores,* "innovators," enemies of traditional religion. Although the Jesuits were anything but Protestants, in some ways they were innovators—for instance, in encouraging the frequent reception of Holy Communion by laypeople, in not singing the divine office in choir, and in not wearing a distinctive habit or uniform of a religious order. The rise of Protestantism made many conservative Catholics suspicious of anything new. The Paris faculty was also committed to upholding Gallican Liberties—France's special role in the Catholic church and its exemptions from papal legislation that the French church had not ratified. The vow that the Jesuit leaders made to go on missions assigned by the pope made them suspect in the eyes of many French churchmen. During Loyola's adult life, France and Spain fought five wars in struggling for European hegemony, and it was in the first of these wars that Ignatius had been wounded. While the early Jesuits were far more international than the twenty other male religious orders founded during the sixteenth century, most of their early leaders were Spanish. That was enough to make many Frenchmen suspicious.

Fortunately King Henry II (ruled 1547–1559) did not share these suspicions and issued a charter authorizing the Jesuits to settle in France and even set up a college in Paris. But the Parlement of Paris, a law court dominated by the nobility, refused to register the royal charter on the grounds that the privileges that Paul III had granted the Jesuits infringed on Gallican Liberties, French sovereignty, and the rights of bishops. In 1553 Henry reexamined the papal bulls given the Jesuits and again authorized the Jesuits. Thereupon the Parlement turned the question over to the theologians of the Sorbonne and to Eustache du

Bellay, the archbishop of Paris, who was also an enemy of the Jesuits. Du Bellay refused to ordain Jesuits or to allow them to preach. In 1554 the theologians at the Sorbonne issued a blistering attack claiming that the Jesuits brought contempt on other religious orders by not singing the office and not employing physical penances. They could not be distinguished from diocesan priests because they did not wear distinctive clothing like the other religious orders. They undermined the jurisdiction of the bishops; they caused turmoil between church and state; they encouraged monks to desert their monasteries; they encouraged contention and jealousy. The Jesuits were even a danger to the faith, men who tore down where they should have been building up. Loyola's response to the verdict of the Sorbonne was to issue orders for Jesuits all over Europe to contact the princes, magistrates, and universities wherever there was a Jesuit community and secure from them statements attesting to the good works and orthodoxy of the Jesuits. These documents were then forwarded to Paris. Some Jesuits urged Loyola to secure from the pope a bull excommunicating the professors of the Sorbonne, but he wisely saw this as counterproductive and an insult to the university he deeply loved. Hostilities began to ease in late August, when the leading French cardinal came to Rome with four Paris theologians, including the author of the university's blistering attack. Loyola arranged for the four to meet with four leading Jesuit theologians and discuss their differences. The eight were able to reach considerable agreement, but opposition at the University of Paris continued. Still, the Jesuits were able to open a college at Clermont-Ferrand in 1556, which quickly enrolled eight hundred students.

The Jesuits had enjoyed excellent relations with the popes from their authorization in 1540 until May 1555, when Cardinal Gianpietro Carafa was elected pope as Paul IV. He was a man of unquestioned zeal but supremely

stubborn. When he was named head of the newly established Roman Inquisition in 1542, he was so eager that he
paid for its start-up costs out of his own pocket. Earlier he
had cofounded the Theatine religious order. As noted already, when he was in Venice, Loyola had composed a cri-
tique of the Theatines that somehow came to Carafa's
knowledge. The two seem to have had a face-to-face con-
frontation that infuriated Carafa. Later Loyola rejected a
proposal to merge the Jesuits and the Theatines. For some
twenty years Carafa had been the bitter opponent of a
group known as the *spirituali,* mainly churchmen led by
cardinals Gasparo Contarini and Giovanni Morone, both
good friends of the Jesuits. Carafa regarded the *spirituali*
as soft on Protestantism, if not themselves infected by
heresy. As pope he moved quickly to have Morone impris-
oned by the Inquisition. Significantly, as soon as Paul IV
died, his successor, Pius IV, not only freed Morone but put
him in charge of reconvening the Council of Trent. Carafa
harbored a hatred for Spaniards because Spain had taken
over his homeland, the Kingdom of Naples. After his election as pope he launched a war against Spain in the impossible dream of liberating his homeland. Here too Pius IV
reversed his policies. Many historians regard Paul IV as
half mad in his old age.

On the eve of the papal election, Loyola asked Jesuits to
pray that the new pope not be a man inclined to change
Jesuit life. Clearly he had Carafa in mind. When the news
of Carafa's election was brought to Loyola, his face fell
and his body began to tremble; he rose and went to the
chapel to pray. When he returned, he had recovered his
usual serenity, confident that divine providence would
prevail despite his worst nightmare having come to pass.

Loyola's first audience with Paul IV went smoothly. The
pope even wanted to make Laínez a cardinal and set aside
a room for him in the papal palace so he could serve as a
theological advisor; Laínez declined both offers. Paul IV

gave not a single coin to help the Roman College. Gradually his suspicions of Spaniards gained the upper hand, and he ordered his troops to search the main Jesuit residence in Rome for hidden arms. Of course they found none. He forced Jesuits to do manual labor in building up the defenses of Rome against a possible Spanish attack that never came. Shortly after Loyola's death Paul IV denounced him as a tyrant in the presence of Laínez, who became the new Jesuit superior general. He also told Laínez that the Jesuits would have to chant the divine office in choir, just as the Theatines and other religious orders did. The Jesuits complied—until Paul died, for his oral command then ceased and the earlier written papal exemptions from choir again took effect.

Popular stereotypes have long depicted the Jesuits as the shock troops of the Counter-Reformation and of resurgent Catholicism against the Protestant reformers. That image is at best a half-truth. As noted earlier, Pedro de Ribadeneira, who published the first biography of Loyola (Latin edition in 1572, revised Spanish edition in 1583), depicted Loyola and Luther as the champions of good and evil religious reform, respectively. The Luther-Loyola antithesis has been popular ever since. Luther, however, would have known little about Loyola. While Loyola certainly was aware of Luther's life and ideas and opposed his teaching, Loyola curiously refers to him by name only once in all his writings and correspondence. Only in small measure can the early Jesuits be seen as a Catholic militia recruited to fight Protestantism. Ignatius and his first companions originally vowed to go to Palestine and work there for the good of souls. Loyola's adult life largely coincided with the reign of Suleiman the Magnificent (1520–1566) and the zenith of the Ottoman Empire, years when Turkish forces generally had the upper hand against Christians. The greatest successes of the early Jesuits and their largest source of recruits were in Portugal and Sicily, which were remote from Germany and hardly touched by Protestant ideas. Both countries were militantly Catholic, but they saw Islam as their main enemy. Several expeditions with Jesuit chaplains, including Laínez, set out from Sicily to fight the Barbary pirates. In July 1550 Loyola sent a letter of encouragement to the Spanish soldiers besieging Tunis under the command of Juan de Vega, the viceroy of Sicily and patron of the Jesuits.

The most militant documents that Ignatius ever wrote were two letters to Father Jerome Nadal in August 1552; Loyola instructed Nadal to pass their contents to Charles V. The first letter made concrete suggestions on how a fleet should be equipped to protect Italy, Sicily, and Spain and patrol the Mediterranean against the Barbary pirates. The second letter is divided into two parts, one of which develops ten ways the emperor could raise money to build and supply a fleet of upwards of three hundred ships, mainly galleys. The financial burden would largely fall on the emperor's Spanish and Italian subjects, especially on church revenues and the nobility, but the emperor could also raise help from his allies, such as the king of Portugal and the Italian cities of Genoa, Lucca, Siena, and Florence. Those cities had lost much more to the Turks and Moorish pirates than the "cost of wiping out the robbers. Let them spend on the fleet what they have been accustomed to spend on defense." Ignatius also suggested nine advantages the fleet would have. Here we note just two of them: first, a fleet would free the coasts of Spain and Italy from chronic losses to pirate raids and would cut the need to maintain garrisons everywhere the raiders might strike. Second, a powerful fleet would also secure mastery of the sea and make it easy for Charles to recapture lands he had lost and make new conquests on the coast of Africa and perhaps also in Greece and the islands of the Mediterranean. Loyola's suggestion went unheeded, for that same year France and the Lutheran princes launched a surprise attacked against Charles V. He lost this war, known as the Second Schmalkaldic War, and was so discouraged that he abdicated and retired to a Spanish monastery. His son Philip took over his possessions in Spain, Italy, the Netherlands, and the New World, while his brother Ferdinand was elected Holy Roman Emperor and received the Austrian lands.

The Peace of Augsburg ended the war in 1555 and allowed the German princes and free cities to choose whether their territory would be Catholic or Lutheran. This did not mean freedom of religion for the people. Most statesmen of the period believed that the stability of the state depended on religious uniformity. Churchmen of whatever denomination believed that only the true religion (that is, their own) should be tolerated. All denominations pleaded for toleration when they did not control the state; once firmly in power, they refused to extend freedom of worship to dissenters.

Ignatius of Loyola was no different, even though he had suffered at the hands of the Inquisition in Alcalá, Salamanca, Paris, Venice, and Rome. For him and the early Jesuits the Inquisition was needed to enforce orthodox belief and preserve civic stability. That did not mean he wanted Jesuits to work for the Inquisition. In June 1555, when the Jesuit provincial superior for Portugal wrote him that King John III wanted two Jesuits to serve as Inquisitors, Loyola faced a hard choice. He did not want Jesuits to serve, but he could not bluntly refuse a king who had been a generous patron of the Jesuits. His reply was not an outright refusal but proposed so many conditions that the king backed away. It is worth noting that Ignatius also used a similar strategy when popes tried to make Borgia and Laínez cardinals. He would allow Jesuits to become bishops but only in missionary countries such as Ethiopia. Undoubtedly the fact that almost all the Inquisitors were friars, mostly

Dominicans, conditioned Loyola's stance: Jesuit Inquisitors would be seen as invading Dominican turf.

In Germany especially, but also in some French and Italian cities, Jesuit preachers attacked Luther and Calvin. They tried to strengthen the Catholic faith among the wavering and win back those who had accepted Protestant teaching. In this they had mixed results. At the Council of Trent Laínez, Salmerón, and Canisius served as papal theologians, and their presentations before the bishops at the council took a hard line against the teachings of Luther and Calvin. But during Loyola's lifetime Jesuits wrote surprisingly few books that tried to refute Protestant teaching. Except for *The Spiritual Exercises,* the most influential Jesuit books of the period were the catechisms of Peter Canisius, which remained popular in Germany for four centuries, but his catechisms rarely even advert explicitly to Protestant teaching.

In September 1549 Loyola wrote instructions on dealing with Protestants that were given to Jesuits leaving Rome to work in Germany. He encouraged the Jesuits to try to make friends with Protestant leaders and win them over by sensitivity and signs of love. They should master the theological questions over which Catholics and Protestants differ so they can strengthen wavering Catholics and defend Catholic teaching in lectures, sermons, and private conversations. But their zeal in countering heresy must show their love for Protestants and sympathy for them, as they too were searching for salvation. The Jesuits should defend papal authority but in a way that does not lose credibility by misguided partisanship.

Loyola's most militant recommendations for dealing with Protestants are found in a letter of August 1554 to Peter Canisius, who was to pass the recommendation on to King Ferdinand. The king should not allow Protestants to serve as governors in his territories or sit on his royal council. Professors or administrators at universities in his territory who attacked Catholic teaching should be ejected from their posts. Students who caused trouble should be expelled. Only Catholics should be allowed to teach in secondary schools. Heretical books should be destroyed and their printing forbidden. Clergymen found teaching heresy should lose their parish and all church income, even if good replacements could not be found: "Better that the flock have no shepherd than have a wolf for a shepherd." Likewise clergy who were orthodox in faith but were ignorant or guilty of public sin should be removed since their bad example fostered heresy. Loyola recommended prison, exile, and even a few executions, but he did not think that setting up an inquisition would be wise in Germany.

To this, his harshest attack on Protestants, he added a long list of positive ways to encourage Catholic belief and practice. Thus students from local Jesuit colleges should spend their Sundays and holidays teaching catechism in the countryside: "Besides correct doctrine they will be giving an example of virtuous living." Loyola also noted that Protestant success was mainly due to their many popular pamphlets and to the bad example and ignorance of Catholic priests. He recommended the writing of a summary of theology that would draw on scripture and tradition to refute contrary teachings. Most needed was an effective catechism for children. Canisius produced his catechism the very next year. Loyola also recommended more Jesuit colleges. King Ferdinand did not implement Loyola's recommendations, either because Canisius did not give them to him or because he feared they would spark unrest at a time when he was losing the Second Schmalkaldic War to the Lutherans.

Finally, Loyola encountered some opposition within the Jesuit Order itself. The most interesting cases involve prophecies about the end of the world. Many books in the New Testament, most notably the Book of Revelation, predict the second coming of Christ and the end of the world, but without clearly indicating when this will take place. From the first century right down to the year 2000, prophets have come forward to predict the imminent end of the world. The most famous case in Loyola's lifetime was at Münster, in Germany, where a group of radical Anabaptists took control of the city in early 1534 and predicted that Christ would return that Easter and make Münster the New Jerusalem. Instead, after a long siege, the city was stormed by a combined Catholic and Lutheran army and the movement's leaders were executed. We have already seen that Loyola forced Guillaume Postel to leave the Jesuits in 1544 when be began making predictions of Christ's second coming. In 1549 a group of three Jesuits (Francis Borgia, Andrés de Oviedo, and François Onfroy) plus a Franciscan (Juan de Tejeda) came together at Gandia. Aside from Borgia, all were mentally unstable. All four believed that the Jesuits needed radical reform and that credence should be given to prophecies of Christ's imminent second coming. Loyola and Polanco, after conferring with other Jesuits in Rome, sent a letter to Borgia in July 1549 that was highly critical of Oviedo and Onfroy and included a long instruction on how to deal with prophecies and spot false prophets. Sensible people might reserve judgment on prophecies that seemed to help spiritual growth but should reject those that contradicted common sense and right theology or did more harm than good.

The differences between Loyola and the four were not limited to the timing of Christ's second coming. The four urged that the time for prayer among the Jesuits should be greatly increased. Oviedo and Borgia wanted eight hours of prayer a day. Both Oviedo and Onfroy asked their superior for permission to spend seven years in solitude so they could prepare their souls for active ministry. Loyola replied to Onfroy that short prayers could be just as effective as long ones and that helping other people is no less a service to God than is prayer. In November 1554 Nadal told Loyola that he had allowed the Spanish Jesuits one and a half hours for prayer. Loyola replied that one hour should be enough for Jesuits in their studies, provided that they were practicing self-denial, though exceptions should, of course, be made for younger Jesuits who were undergoing special spiritual stress. In a letter of June 1551 he urged that Jesuits in training should not devote long hours to meditation, since one hour a day plus daily Mass would suffice; instead they should seek to find God in all things—in their walks, in what they heard and saw, and in all their actions. His letter continues, "One can often offer God our Lord his studies and the work they require since we undertake them out of love for him at the sacrifice of our own personal tastes." Obviously he was here looking back to his own experience in Barcelona, when too much prayer hindered progress in his studies.

XV

Loyola's Roman Writings

After his many years of travel Loyola settled in Rome from 1537 until his death in 1556. During those nineteen years he wrote three important works: he kept a spiritual diary, dictated a short autobiography covering 1521 to 1538, and wrote the Constitutions of the Jesuit Order. These works were not as influential outside the order as *The Spiritual Exercises* were, but all three help reveal the man and the values that drove him.

The earliest of the three was his spiritual diary, which may well have covered all his years in Rome. Toward the end of his life he showed a large bundle of spiritual notes to Luis Gonçalves da Câmara, to whom he was dictating his autobiography. Gonçalves asked to read them, but Loyola refused. He was very private about his spiritual experiences, and later he apparently destroyed his diary except for two short folders of notes that escaped his attention. They are the longest example we have of his own handwriting and provide our best evidence about his prayer life during his Roman years. Although two early biographers recorded a few paragraphs from them, these notes escaped attention until their publication in 1892. The first folder covers 2 February to 12 March 1544; the second, shorter folder covers 13 March 1544 to 27 February 1545, and the whole text covers only forty pages in a modern edition. The first folder reveals Loyola wrestling with whether the Jesuit Constitutions should allow Professed Houses to have a fixed income or make them rely on begging and freewill offerings. The Professed Houses normally were residences where Jesuit priests lived as a community and included a church where they preached, administered the sacraments, and directed people through the Spiritual Exercises.

Loyola's deliberations followed two procedures that he had proposed in the Exercises. There he advised persons making key decisions about their lives to reflect rationally on the advantages and disadvantages of one alternative, then to do the same for the other alternative. They should make up their mind "according to the stronger movement of reason and not through any sensual inclination." But that was not enough—they must search for God's confirmation of that rational decision through prayer and God's working in their hearts. Loyola listed ten reasons why Professed Houses should have a fixed income to cover their expenses. The reasons are pragmatic: for instance, Jesuits would not have to spend time badgering people for alms and would have more time for study, preaching, and other ministries. Buildings would be cleaner and better kept up. He then listed sixteen reasons why they should not have any fixed income: for instance, Jesuits would have to put their whole trust in God, would be more diligent in helping others and bearing hardship, and would be kept humble by begging. Loyola finally decided that the Professed Houses should have no fixed income. Most of his spiritual diary records what he saw as God working in his heart to confirm that decision by filling him with spiritual consolations, tears of joy, and mystical experiences. His spiritual diary provides the best surviving evidence about the mystical dimensions of Loyola's Roman years.

Mystical experiences are as difficult to define as explaining colors to a blind person. To nonbelievers they seem no more than self-delusion. Yet mysticism has a large role not only in the historic spirituality of Christians (whether Catholics, Orthodox, or Protestants) but also of Jews, Muslims, Buddhists, and Hindus. Mysticism is a direct and deeply personal experience of the Ultimate that surpasses reason or the senses. In Western religious traditions mystical experience is not something that people can attain by their own striving—rather God comes down and sweeps them up.

Loyola's experiences usually took the form of contentment and tears of joy and were tied to his celebration of Mass. His daily entries usually note deep consolation, which he saw as God's confirmation of his decision to embrace total poverty. But this was not always the case. Thus upon arising on 18 February 1544 he was sluggish and found no relish in prayer and began to wonder whether he had made the right decision, but as he continued praying he regained his usual relish and joy. On February 19 during his mass he shed tears of joy and felt he had deep insights into the mystery of the Trinity that he could not have gained by hard study through his whole lifetime. Later that day, while walking the city streets, whenever he saw three objects together, whether people or animals or other things, his mind went back to the Trinity. Three days later in preparing for mass he somehow felt that Christ was present and was confirming the decision for strictest poverty.

The second set of notes, covering 13 March 1544 to 27 February 1545, are much thinner and have many gaps—days and weeks with no entries—and the entries tend to be much shorter. The focus of his prayer was no longer whether Professed Houses should have no fixed income, but his experiences of God were still usually linked to his celebration of mass in a tiny chapel adjacent to his living quarters.

The diary suggests that Loyola's mystical experiences were comparable to those of other giants of the golden age of Spanish mysticism, Saint Teresa of Avila (1515–1582) and Saint John of the Cross (1542–1591), but they were gifted writers who wanted to explain the nature of mystical experience. Ignatius did not have their literary skill, and his spiritual diaries contain only short and unsystematic entries meant for his eyes alone. The mysticism of all three, unlike that of many *alumbrados,* was not a private road to God that ignored or replaced scripture, the Trinity, Christ, and the sacraments of the church. Rather, their mysticism was tied to and built upon traditional Christian teaching and practice.

Loyola's spiritual diary reveal his inner life during his Roman years. Our main source for his earlier years is his autobiography, which is sometimes called his acts or reminiscences and covers the years 1521 to 1538. Loyola's followers were understandably anxious to know as much as possible about his life, but Loyola repeatedly rebuffed requests that he leave behind an account. The founders of religious orders from the Middle Ages onward usually became canonized saints who were held up as patrons and models to be imitated by their religious order. Loyola's awareness of this seems a major reason why he long resisted the attempts of Jerome Nadal, Pedro de Ribadeneira, and Luis Gonçalves da Câmara to have him write or dictate an account of his life. A major theme in the Spiritual Exercises is that honor leads to pride. Loyola's own greatest temptation, as his autobiography makes clear, was to pride and vainglory, and it was probably fear of vainglory that made Loyola so hesitant to provide an account of his life.

Nadal tells us that in 1552, when he saw Loyola's declining health and feared that he might soon die, he begged Ignatius to provide an account that "could serve as a testament and paternal instruction." Nadal was convinced that Loyola "could do nothing of more good for the Society than this." Loyola finally agreed and asked Gonçalves to help him. He probably chose Gonçalves, a Portuguese of noble ancestry, because he was known for his good memory and because he would be readily available since he was serving as subsuperior in the Roman community. In three time blocks—August and September 1552, March 1555, and September and October 1555,— Ignatius invited Gonçalves into his room and paced the floor as he related his life story. Ignatius chose these months because his other work was less pressing and his health was better. Gonçalves wrote a short account of how he would listen to Ignatius, then go to his room and write down notes on what Loyola had said; later he polished his notes and dictated them to a secretary in Spanish. The last section had to be dictated in Italian because no Spanish-speaking secretary was available. Like most autobiographies of the Renaissance, Loyola's is written in the third person. Loyola calls himself "the pilgrim," probably because much of his account is devoted to his pilgrimage to Jerusalem, but also because he saw his whole life as a pilgrimage to God. Loyola's narrative is often vivid but sometimes obscure.

Loyola stressed how naive and yet generous he was after his conversion. Thus in his encounter with the Moor, he left it up to his donkey to decide whether he would kill the Moor or let him go. In traveling to Jerusalem he gave away all his money because bringing money for expenses seemed to question God's providence. Late in life he regretted the fasting and self-scourging he had done at Manresa, because he had injured his health and thereby hurt his ability to help others. In the Jesuit Constitutions he discouraged severe penances so that his men could use their good health for the service of God and neighbor.

Loyola's autobiography breaks off abruptly in 1538, soon after his arrival in Rome. His last sentence to

Gonçalves was "The other things Master Nadal will be able to recount." There seem three reasons for the abrupt ending: Gonçalves was just about to leave Rome for Portugal; Ignatius knew that Jerome Nadal and other close associates could give details about his Roman years, and finally Loyola was a private person who did not like to talk about his own experiences. That is why he had put off dictating his autobiography and destroyed most of his spiritual diary. Many of the external details of his life found in the autobiography can be confirmed from other sources, but for his inward thoughts and development, so central to who he was, historians are dependant on his own narrative. Few autobiographies of the sixteenth century have been reprinted as often as his.

The Constitutions of the Jesuit Order are a much longer work of greater historical importance than Loyola's autobiography and the extant fragments of his diary. As has been noted, the early companions commissioned Loyola and Jean Codure to draw up constitutions, but Codure died in 1541, and Loyola postponed work on the Constitutions, partly because of his other work but also because by waiting he could draw on the lived experience of Jesuits rather than try to write the Constitutions from some abstract master plan. Later his deteriorating health slowed work on the Constitutions, but the appointment of Juan Polanco as his secretary in March 1547 proved a turning point in this work. Both the Spanish draft of the Constitutions and the later official Latin text were written by Polanco in a style superior to Loyola's, but all the crucial decisions about content were made by Loyola himself. Ignatius asked Polanco to secure copies of the rules of previous religious orders and (as noted earlier) the constitutions of many universities. Loyola went over them and borrowed ideas, discarding what he felt did not fit with the Formula, the preliminary statement of the society's purpose that he and his companions had presented to Paul

III. In writing the Constitutions, Loyola often had Polanco draw up a list of reasons for and against various options on which decisions had to be reached. Loyola would reflect and pray over the options and then make his final decision. By the end of 1550 the draft of the Constitutions was well along, so Loyola gathered the senior Jesuit priests working near Rome and submitted it for their suggestions and approval. He also asked to resign as general superior of the order so that he could do missionary work in Africa. They gave general approval to the Constitutions but rejected his resignation.

When finally approved and published, the Constitutions differed greatly from the classic rules of previous religious orders, those of Saints Basil, Augustine, Benedict, and Francis. Those rules were relatively short and contained more exhortation than specific legislation. The Jesuit Constitutions are much longer, 264 pages with footnotes in the standard modern English translation, and many contain detailed regulations.

Aside from Polanco, Jerome Nadal was Loyola's most trusted subordinate in his last five years. In March 1552 Loyola gave him a draft of the Constitutions to promulgate, explain, and implement in Sicily. Nadal then reported back to him and presented the reactions to the new regulations, which were still a work in progress. In April 1553 Ignatius sent Nadal to Spain and Portugal to promulgate the Constitutions. In February 1555 Nadal began the same task in Germany. Obviously Loyola did not want the Constitutions suddenly imposed on Jesuits worldwide without their input. Minor adjustments and polishing, based on local feedback, were still in process when Loyola died in 1556.

The Jesuit Constitutions have an introduction and then the ten parts of the Constitutions proper. The introduction includes the Formula of the Institute, which Ignatius and his companions drew up in 1539. It was incorporated in the papal bulls which gave official approval to the order. The introduction also includes the General Examen, a set

Ignatius holding the Constitutions.

of questions put to men interested in joining the society; the Examen also describes for them the purpose of the society.

The first five parts of the Constitutions proper describe how men are to be admitted to the Society, why they may decide to leave or be asked to leave, and the spiritual and intellectual development expected of members. The sixth part takes up the three vows of poverty, chastity, and obedience traditionally taken by members of religious orders.

The seventh part of the Constitutions discusses the various missions or tasks that Jesuits were to perform. The choice of tasks should always be determined by what is "for the greater glory of God." The eighth part tackles ways to tie together Jesuit communities scattered throughout the world, for instance, by sending Rome letters that summarized their work every four months. These letters would help the superior general to keep abreast of developments wherever Jesuits lived around the world. The ninth part of the Constitutions outlines the duties of the superior general (often simply called the general) and the qualities he should possess. He should combine gentleness with the ability to act decisively, even severely, when circumstances demand it. The general was given sweeping powers not found in previous religious orders; most important, he appointed all other important superiors. The general was elected for life by a General Congregation, the society's supreme governing body made up of the provincial superior and elected delegates from each province of the society. The tenth and last part of the Constitutions discusses ways the order could preserve and develop its well-being.

Several aspects of the Jesuit Constitutions need emphasis. Authority and decision making were centralized in the general, who served for life, unlike the heads of other religious orders. Most orders had general congregations that met regularly, whereas Jesuit General Congregations met only to elect a new general or when the general himself decided to call a General Congregation because of urgent business. Various reasons have been suggested as to why Loyola chose to centralize authority in one man. Probably the main reasons were that centralized authority made for greater efficiency and that a rapid turnover of generals might hinder steady control. Moreover, the general would have difficulty in reforming communities that elected their own superiors since lax communities would tend to elect lax superiors, who in turn would prevent effective reform. The centralized authority of the Jesuits based in Rome also made it difficult for secular rulers to interfere with the order's internal government. The rulers of France and Spain, for instance, controlled the appointment of Benedictine abbots. The appointment of all important superiors by the Jesuit general precluded this sort of royal intervention. Although the Constitutions can be very specific on many points—for instance, regulations concerning Jesuit schools—Loyola well knew how dangerous it was to try to control everything from Rome, especially in an age when information moved slowly. He therefore repeatedly added the caution that the application of general norms must be adapted to particular places, persons, and circumstances.

Unlike other religious orders whose members shared equal status and rights, Loyola set up several different grades among the Jesuits. Men entering the Jesuits spent two years as novices during which they learned about Jesuit life and made the Spiritual Exercises. After two years they pronounced simple perpetual vows of poverty, chastity, and obedience. Members of most other religious orders changed their names when they entered or took vows; Jesuits retained their original family names for life. Entrants could aim at being either priests or lay brothers. About a quarter became brothers, and immediately after taking their vows they were assigned jobs within Jesuit communities such as cook, nurse, secretary, or janitor. Those destined for the priesthood were called scholastics and began long years of studies that included classical languages and literature, philosophy, and theology. Usually they were assigned to teach at Jesuit colleges for a few years before studying theology. On completing theology they were ordained as priests.

An elite called Professed Fathers also made a special fourth vow to go on any mission that the pope assigned them. Thus Pope Paul III sent Xavier to India and Salmerón and Broët to Ireland. In fact only a tiny number of Jesuits were ever sent on such missions by popes. This vow has often been wrongly seen as binding all Jesuits to blind obedience to the papacy on all issues, but Jesuits did stress loyalty to the pope. Tens of thousands of Jesuits over the centuries were sent on missions, often to distant lands and on dangerous assignments, but it was the Jesuit general or local superiors, not the pope, who sent them.

In his comparative study of the rules of religious orders, the distinguished British historian David Knowles noted that although Loyola always treated his men as individuals, from the perspective of their Constitutions the Jesuits "must be regarded as the most carefully centralized and disciplined non-military body that ever existed." Knowles even claims that in the Reformation era almost all Protestants and many Catholics were so hostile to religious orders that the success of the Jesuits saved religious orders from disappearing in the Catholic church, and that they provided the pattern for almost all orders and congregations of active life established during the next three centuries.

The Jesuit Constitutions combine legislation with the spirituality of the Spiritual Exercises. Monastic orders centered on the personal sanctification of the monks. The medieval orders of friars, such as the Dominicans and Franciscans, balanced personal sanctification with active ministry. The Jesuit Constitutions did not see personal sanctification and ministry for the spiritual and temporal good of people as two separate goals. They were to be interlocking and mutually reinforcing. Jesuits were to be contemplatives in action who did not withdraw from the world but sought to find God in all things, especially in the people they were working with. Monks traditionally took a vow of stability—a commitment to live out their lives in a particular monastery. The Jesuit Constitutions stressed that Jesuits should be ready to travel to all parts of the world. The exception was Loyola himself, chained to his desk in Rome. But that was precisely what his service of God and of his brethren demanded. Juan Polanco noted that even in his days as a courtier Ignatius had certain special talents from God: "Above all he was very eager in taking on demanding tasks, persistent in carrying them out and wise in seeing them through to completion." Nowhere were these same gifts more evident than in his last major task, writing the Jesuit Constitutions.

XVI

Going Home

Loyola's death on 31 July 1556 was the result of health problems that had plagued him for many years. The severe penances he performed at Manresa harmed his health, and bad health forced him to cut short his theological studies at Paris and return to Spain. After leaving Spain he tried again to study theology at the University of Bologna, but ill health forced him to go to Venice, where he improved. Since there was no university in Venice, he had to study theology on his own while he waited for his companions to gather for their projected voyage to Palestine. Loyola enjoyed fairly good health during his first decade in Rome, but in May 1548 his health started to decline. He had eight more years to live, but they were punctuated by periods of illness (July and December 1548; January 1549; December 1550; January 1551; September and October 1553; April, June through August, and November 1554; January and December 1555; and January 1556). In June 1553 he almost died, and his health was so bad in November 1554 that Jerome Nadal was named vicar general to carry out the work Loyola could not manage. There were, of course, other interludes of comparatively good health.

On 2 July 1556 Ignatius left Rome and went to the countryside villa of the Roman College in hopes of recovery. His health did not improve at the villa, so he was carried back to Rome on July 27. He was convinced that he was dying, but the key Jesuits in Rome had seen him survive so many previous crises that they were more concerned about the health of Diego Laínez, whose life seemed to be in even greater peril. On July 29 Ignatius asked Polanco to have one of the Jesuits who was a doctor check his health, and this was done. The next day Ignatius, convinced that death was at hand, asked Polanco to go and obtain a final blessing from the pope, even though the doctor did not seem worried. Polanco asked Ignatius if he could postpone getting the pope's blessing until he completed some letters that had to be sent to Spain that same day. Ignatius told him to use his own judgment. At dawn on July 31 it was clear that Ignatius was dying, and the lay brother who attended Ignatius searched the house in vain for his confessor. Ignatius died just before seven in the morning without receiving the last sacraments normally given to dying Catholics.

Realdo Colombo, a leading doctor, performed the autopsy on the corpse. In his book on anatomy published in 1559 he writes that he extracted countless gallstones from Loyola's liver, kidneys, lungs, and portal vein. Old age is seldom easy; Loyola's must have been excruciating. Still he carried on his work without complaint right to the end.

Throughout his life Loyola had refused to sit for portraits. A respected painter, Jacopino del Conte, had been one of Loyola's penitents; he seems to have been invited on the day of Loyola's death to make a sketch from the corpse; from it he later made the painting that is widely regarded as the best portrait of Ignatius. A plaster death mask was made; a copy of this was sent to Alonso Sánchez Coello, Philip II's court painter, who based a portrait of Loyola on it.

Jacopino del Conte, who knew Loyola well, painted this portrait from a sketch he made the day of Loyola's death.

Loyola's funeral was held the evening after his death in the Jesuit Church of Sancta Maria della Strada. Hundreds came to say farewell to a man widely regarded as a saint; some in the crowd pushed forward to kiss his hands or his feet or press their rosaries against his body. Precautions were needed to prevent people from clipping off parts of his clothing as relics.

Loyola's body was initially buried near the altar of the same church. The church was small and crumbling, and Loyola had started plans for its replacement in 1554. The great Michelangelo had inspected the site and started work on a model for a new and larger church, but eventually the main architects of the new church were Giocomo della Porta and Jacopo Barozzi. The cornerstone of the church, named the Gesù ("*Jesus*" in Italian), was laid in 1568. Built on the site of Sancta Maria della Strada, a few yards from the building in which Loyola worked and died, the Gesù is widely regarded as a pioneer work in the development of the baroque style. Loyola's body was moved to the new church and buried under a grandiose altar to the left of the nave. A gold-clad baroque statue of Loyola stands gesticulating above the altar. To its right is an allegorical group of statues by Pierre le Gros: the central figure is Faith, who holds a cross and stamps her foot on a fallen male figure who represents Heresy and grips two books with his right arm. Each book has an author's name on its spine: Martin Luther and John Calvin. One suspects that Loyola, who loved simplicity, would have shuddered had he risen from his tomb and looked around the Gesù.

Ignatius was sixty-five at his death—a long lifetime by sixteenth-century standards. His two enduring legacies were *The Spiritual Exercises* and the Society of Jesus. As we have seen, his little book has enjoyed more than 5,000 editions since its publication in 1548 and has been translated into all the major languages of the world. It continues to inspire countless people. The Jesuits run retreat houses in many countries where people can still make the Exercises in abbreviated form.

For two years a war between Paul IV and Philip II prevented the leading Jesuits from meeting to elect Loyola's successor. The First General Congregation elected Diego Laínez as superior general and gave official approval to the Constitutions in 1558. At Loyola's death there were roughly a thousand Jesuits scattered in seventy communities: twenty-four in Italy, twenty in Spain, six in Portugal, two in France, seven in Germany, six in India, three in Brazil, and two in Japan. There were 8,519 Jesuits by 1600 and 19,998 by 1700. Thereafter expansion slowed sharply. During the Enlightenment hostility toward organized religion in general and Jesuits in particular grew among the intellectual elite of Catholic Europe. Several of the absolute monarchs and their advisers saw the traditional Jesuit loyalty to the papacy as a hindrance to their own control of churches and religion. First Portugal, then the Bourbon monarchies of Spain, France, and Naples exiled the Jesuits and confiscated their schools. They put such pressure on Pope Clement XIV that he issued a decree in 1773 suppressing the Jesuit order but without condemning it. The suppression was to take effect when the decree was promulgated by local rulers. Ironically, the two important rulers who did not allow its promulgation were Frederick the Great and Catherine the Great, so the Jesuits continued to teach in Protestant Prussia and Orthodox Russia. The Romantic movement of the early nineteenth century was accompanied by a religious revival, and the French Revolution and Napoleon overturned the power of the Bourbons. Gradually small Jesuit communities were allowed to reopen in several countries, for instance, in the United States in 1805. In 1814 Pius VII authorized the worldwide restoration of the Jesuit Order. For the next 150 years the Jesuits grew worldwide, surpassing their numbers before the suppression although never achieving the influence they enjoyed during the Reformation and Baroque eras. Their growth peaked in the 1960s, when slow decline set in, first in Europe, then in the United States, although they continue to grow in Asia, especially

India, and in Africa. They remain today the largest male religious order and operate twenty universities in the United States, plus colleges, high schools, and parishes.

A Note on the Sources

Very few people of the sixteenth century have left more information about their lives or have been so closely examined by historians as Ignatius Loyola. The major bibliography on Jesuit history, though restricted to items published between 1900 and 1980, is L. Polgar, *Bibliographie sur l'histoire del la Compagnie de Jésus* (Rome: Jesuit Historical Institute, 1981–1990), 6 vols. The first volume lists 1,740 publications dealing with Loyola. Polgar's bibliography is annually updated in the *Archivum Historicum Societatis Iesu*. It is safe to say that no one has read all the books and articles on Loyola. The largest number are in Spanish, but English is second, with French and German close behind. This bibliographic essay emphasizes books available in English.

Biographies of Ignatius Loyola

The most readable short biography is Philip Caraman's *Ignatius Loyola: A Biography of the Founder of the Jesuits* (San Francisco: Harper and Row, 1990). Cándido de Dalmases's *Ignatius of Loyola, Founder of the Jesuits: His Life and Work*, translated by Jerome Aixalá (St. Louis: Institute of Jesuit Sources, 1985), is meticulous, concise, and dry. Mary Purcell's *The First Jesuit: St. Ignatius Loyola* (Chicago: Loyola University Press, 1981), is aimed at a more popular audience. J. Ignacio Tellechea Idígoras, a leading Spanish church historian, has written a stylish longer biography: *Ignatius of Loyola: The Pilgrim Saint*, translated by Cornelius M. Buckley (Chicago: Loyola University Press, 1994). *St. Ignatius Loyola* (London: Collins, 1979), by Karl Rahner and Paul Imhoff, provides a rich collection of color pictures and old engravings illustrating Loyola's life. Still useful is James Brodrick's *St. Ignatius Loyola: The Pilgrim Years, 1491–1538* (New York: Farrar, Straus and Company, 1956). Brodrick was an excellent stylist, but his biography stops just before the foundation of the Jesuits. He tells that story in his *The Origin of the Jesuits* (London: Longan, 1940). Readers interested in psychobiography should examine W. W. Meissner's *The Psychology of a Saint: Ignatius of Loyola* (New Haven: Yale University Press, 1992).

Most of the authors noted so far are Catholics and many are Jesuits. For a sympathetic Protestant view Paul van Dyke's *Ignatius of Loyola: The Founder of the Jesuits* (New York: Scribner's Sons, 1926) is still useful. The best hostile interpretation is Ludwig Marcuse's *Soldier of Christ: the Life of Ignatius Loyola,* translated by Christopher Lazare (New York: Simon and Schuster, 1939). Marcuse possesses a lively style and knows the sources. For him Loyola was gradually corrupted by a thirst for power over people: "Kings, businessmen and the monk imperialist must think only of conquering the world. . . . A cross fertilization of the seed [of Francis] of Assisi and Machiavelli. And Machiavelli was the stronger."

Ignatius Loyola's main contribution to history was the founding of the Jesuits. This aspect of his work is studied by André Ravier, *Ignatius of Loyola and the Founding of the Society of Jesus*, translated by Maura, Joan, and Carson Daly (San Francisco: Ignatius Press, 1987). David Knowles provides the historical context for the Jesuit Constitutions in *From Pa-*

chomius to Ignatius: A Study on the Constitutional History of Religious Orders (Oxford: Clarendon Press, 1960). As noted earlier, Ribadeneira's pioneer biography of Loyola contrasted Loyola with Martin Luther; a modern development of this theme is Friedrich Richter's *Martin Luther and Ignatius Loyola: Spokesmen for Two Worlds of Belief* (Westminster, MD: Newman Press, 1960). Marjorie O'Rourke Boyle's *Loyola's Acts: The Rhetoric of the Self* (Berkeley and Los Angeles: University of California Press, 1997) examines Loyola's autobiography more as a literary construct than as a historical account. A play by L. Michael Bellafiore, *Ignatius of Loyola: The Story of the Pilgrim* (2002), is available on video (contact <www.loyolapress.org>).

Loyola's Spirituality

Joseph de Guibert's *The Jesuits: Their Spiritual Doctrine and Practice,* translated by William J. Young (Chicago: Loyola University Press, 1964), puts Loyola's own spirituality (pp. 1–181) in the context of later developments. Equally valuable is Hugo Rahner's *The Spirituality of St. Ignatius Loyola: An Account of Its Historical Development,* translated by F. J. Smith (Chicago: Loyola University Press, 1980). Harvey Egan's *Ignatius Loyola the Mystic* (Wilmington, DE: Michael Glazier, 1987) studies this key aspect of his life. For Loyola's impact on later spirituality, see the collection of essays edited by Friedrich Wulf, *Ignatius Loyola, His Personality and Spiritual Heritage, 1556–1956* (St. Louis: Institute of Jesuit Sources, 1977). Joseph Conwell's *Impelling Spirit: Revisiting the Founding Spirit: 1539, Ignatius of Loyola and his Companions* (Chicago: Loyola University Press, 1997) explores how Loyola affected the men closest to him. A short introduction to his spirituality is David Lonsdale's *Eyes to See, Ears to Hear: An Introduction to Ignatian Spirituality* (Chicago: Loyola University Press, 1990). William Meissner in his *To the Greater Glory—A Psychological Study of Ignatian Spirituality* (Milwaukee: Marquette University Press, 1999) uses the insights of modern psychology to enrich our understanding of the Spiritual Exercises. Katherine Dyckman, Mary Gavin, and Elizabeth Liebert explore how to adapt the Spiritual Exercises for women of today in *The Spiritual Exercises Reclaimed: Uncovering Liberating Possibilities for Women* (Mahwah, N J: Paulist Press, 2001).

The Jesuit Impact on Education and Culture

Loyola did not initially expect Jesuits to be teachers, but within a generation of his death most Jesuits were working in education, and this has been their most important ministry ever since. George Ganss's *St. Ignatius' Idea of a Jesuit University* (Milwaukee: Marquette University Press, 1956) shows how he laid the foundations of this development. The best overview of the Jesuit impact on the arts and sciences is the essays collected in John W. O'Malley et al., editors, *The Jesuits: Cultures, Sciences and the Arts, 1540–1773* (Toronto: Toronto University Press, 1999).

Loyola's Companions

"No man is an island." Ignatius Loyola was influential mainly because he gathered around him a group of gifted companions. Many of these have been subjects of good biographies. The best comprehensive study of these men is John W. O'Malley's *The First Jesuits* (Cambridge, MA: Harvard University Press, 1993). Still useful is Javier Osuna's *Friends in the Lord: A Study in the Origins and Growth of Community in the Society of Jesus,* translated by N. King (London: The Way, 1974). There are many biographies of Francis Xavier; the most readable is James Brodrick's, *Saint Francis Xavier* (New York: Wicklow Press, 1952). Less readable but more detailed are the four massive volumes of Georg Schurhammer's *Francis Xavier: His Life, His Times,* translated by M. Joseph Costelloe (Rome: Jesuit Historical Institute, 1973–1982); the first volume has valuable details on

Loyola's life in Paris and in Italy before 1540. William Bangert, in addition to his *A History of the Society of Jesus* (St. Louis: Institute of Jesuit Sources, 1986), has written biographies of four of Loyola's early companions: *To the Other Towns: A Life of Blessed Peter Favre* (Westminster, MD: Newman Press, 1959), *Claude Jay and Alphonso Salmeron: Two Early Jesuits* (Chicago, Loyola University Press, 1985), and (with Thomas McCoog) *Jerome Nadal, S.J., 1507–1580: Tracking the First Generation of Jesuits* (Chicago: Loyola University Press, 1992). For Francis Borgia, see Cándido de Dalmases, *Francis Borgia, Grandee of Spain, Jesuit, Saint,* translated by Michael Buckley (St. Louis: Institute of Jesuit Sources, 1991).

General Background

The literature on the Reformation era is immense. Two recent surveys are James Tracy's *Europe's Reformations, 1450–1650* (Lanham, MD: Rowman and Littlefield, 1999) and Carter Lindberg's *The European Reformations* (Oxford: Blackwell, 1996). For an interpretation of Catholicism in this era, see Robert Bireley's *The Refashioning of Catholicism, 1450–1700* (Washington, DC: Catholic University Press, 1999). A classic interpretation of the Counter-Reformation, which devotes a chapter to the Spiritual Exercises, is H. Outram Evennett's *The Spirit of the Counter-Reformation,* edited by John Bossy (Cambridge, UK: Cambridge University Press, 1968). More comprehensive are *Handbook of European History, 1400–1600: Late Middle Ages, Renaissance and Reformation,* edited by Thomas Brady et al. (Leiden, The Nether lands: E. J. Brill, 1994–1995), 2 vols., and *The Oxford Encyclopedia of the Reformation,* edited by Hans J. Hillerbrand (New York: Oxford University Press, 1996), 4 vols. John O'Malley has gathered bibliographic essays by specialists in *Catholicism in Early Modern Europe: A Guide to Research* (St. Louis: Center for Reformation Research, 1988).

Primary Sources

Polanco: The Writings of St. Ignatius of Loyola in Comput-erized Form is a CD-ROM, that gives the full texts of all Loyola's writings in their original language and includes all his letters, together with an explanatory manual and search engines. It is available from the Institute of Jesuit Sources (3700 W. Pine Blvd., St. Louis, MO, 63108). Critical editions of Loyola's writings and primary sources about his life are available in the *Monumenta Historica Societatis Iesu* (Madrid/Rome: Institutum Historicum Societatis Iesu, 1894–), an enormous series of interest mainly to specialists. Twenty-nine volumes deal directly with Loyola: twelve vol-umes of his letters, three dealing with the Spiritual Exercises, four with the Jesuit Constitutions, and four with narrative sources. Six more volumes print Juan Polanco's chronicle of the Jesuits, 1539–1556. Still other volumes in the series deal with Loyola's companions and their correspondence.

There are two fine collections of Loyola's writings in Eng-lish. The handiest is *Saint Ignatius of Loyola: Personal Writ-ings*, translated and edited by Joseph A. Munitiz and Philip Endean (London: Penguin Books, 1996); it contains Loyola's autobiography, his spiritual diary, *The Spiritual Exercises*, and forty of his letters. *Ignatius of Loyola: The Spiritual Ex-ercises and Selected Works,* edited by George Ganss (Mah-wah, NJ: Paulist Press, 1991), contains the same works plus selected passages from the Jesuit Constitutions, but it in-cludes only ten letters. George Ganss has also edited and translated the full text of the Jesuit Constitutions in. *The Constitutions of the Society of Jesus* (St. Louis: Institute of Jesuit Sources, 1970). Many other English translations of the autobiography and *The Spiritual Exercises* are available.

Three useful collections of Loyola's correspondence are those edited by William Young, *Letters of St. Ignatius of Loyola* (Chicago: Loyola University Press, 1959); by Joseph Tylenda, *Counsels for Jesuits: Selected Letters and Instruc-tions of Saint Ignatius Loyola* (Chicago: Loyola University Press, 1985), which presents forty letters of spiritual advice to Jesuits; and by Hugo Rahner, *Saint Ignatius Loyola: Letters to Women*, translated by K. Pound and S. A. H. Weetman (New York: Herder and Herder, 1960). Rahner's introduction gives a fine overview of Loyola's correspondence.

No organization of comparable size contributed as much as the Jesuits did to the exchange of information and ideas around the world—in short, to globalization—during the sixteenth and seventeenth centuries. The original goal of Loyola and his companions, to work in Palestine, was frustrated by war. As was noted, during his lifetime the Jesuits established missions in Brazil, Africa, India, Indonesia, and Japan. Xavier died trying to enter China. The influence of Western civilization on Asia, Africa, and the Americas has been greater than their influence on the West, but their influence has been far greater than most Europeans and Americans realize. The most detailed single study of Asia's contribution to Western culture and economic development is Donald Lach's massive (nine volumes) *Asia in the Making of Europe* (Chicago: University of Chicago Press, 1965–1993). The Jesuits pop up almost everywhere; for example Volume I, Parts I–II, has 472 entries in the index, plus those for individual Jesuits. The pioneer of adapting Jesuit missionary methods to the enormously rich cultural traditions of China was Matteo Ricci (1552–1610); somewhat unconventional but very rewarding is Jonathan Spence's *The Memory Palace of Matteo Ricci* (New York: Viking, 1984). For Ricci's own account of his years in China, see *China in the Sixteenth Century: The Journals of Matteo Ricci, 1583–1610,* translated by Louis Gallagher, (New York: Random House, 1942). A useful collection of essays on the Jesuits in China is *East Meets West: The Jesuits in China, 1582–1773* edited by Charles Ronan and Bonnie Oh (Chicago: Loyola University Press, 1988). The Jesuit contribution to the interaction of western and Chinese philosophy, science, and religion is traced by D. E. Mungello in *Curious Land: Jesuit Accommodation and the Origins of Sinology* (Honolulu: University of Hawaii, 1989).

After the death of Francis Xavier the great planner and co-ordinator of Jesuit mission work in India, Indonesia, Japan, and China was Alessandro Valignano (1539–1606). Josef Franz Schütte's *Valignano's Mission Principles for Japan*, translated by John Coyne (St. Louis: Institute of Jesuit Sources, 1980), provides valuable insight into Jesuit methods for converting non-Europeans in a sophisticated culture. Initially Jesuit missionary work in Japan enjoyed great success, but that very success so alarmed Japanese rulers that they launched the most bitter persecution of Christians in history: that tragic story is related by Charles R. Boxer, *The Christian Century in Japan* (Berkeley and Los Angeles: University of California Press, 1951). The most moving account of the Japanese persecution is found in Shusaku Endo's novel *Silence* (Tokyo: Kodansha International, 1982), translated by William Johnston. The television miniseries *Shogun* (available on video, 1980) is based on James Clavell's novel and depicts the hostility toward Jesuit missionaries of an English sailor shipwrecked in feudal Japan.

For a good introduction to the largely abortive Jesuit mission to Ethiopia, see Philip Caraman's *The Lost Empire: The Story of the Jesuits in Ethiopia, 1555–1634* (South Bend, IN: Notre Dame University Press, 1985). Equally valuable is Caraman's *The Lost Paradise: The Jesuit Republic in South America* (New York: Seabury Press, 1976), which describes the Jesuit reductions in Paraguay. The challenges faced by the early Jesuits working among Native Americans come alive in Claudio Burgaleta's *José de Acosta, S.J. (1540–1600): His Life and Thought* (Chicago: Loyola University Press, 1999). Acosta wrote three noteworthy books: one was in Latin on procuring the salvation of Indians; his *Natural and Moral History of the Indies* (Durham: Duke University Press, 2002) reflects on his fifteen years of work in Peru and Mexico and describes an enormous range of Indian beliefs and customs, and he also wrote a catechism for Native Americans that was printed in Spanish and two different Indian languages in 1585. His catechism and that Valignano wrote for the Japanese are fascinating to compare with the two most popular Jesuit catechisms written for Europeans, those of Saint Peter Canisius and of Saint Robert Bellarmine. In the 1570s Acosta strongly encouraged a reduction, a separate community for some 14,000 Christian Indians, at Juli near today's border between Peru and Bolivia. He insisted that the Jesuits working with the Indians learn their languages. Perhaps the best movie on the Jesuits, *The Mission* (1986), vividly portrays the destruction of Jesuit reductions in Brazil by the Portuguese government, engineered by the marquis de Pombal, who largely controlled royal policy. Pombal shared hostility toward Christianity with many intellectuals of the Enlightenment and wanted government control of church affairs in Portugal; he saw the Jesuits as the chief opponents of his policy. In 1759 he secured the expulsion of all Jesuits from Portugal and its colonies.

Selections from the seventy-three volumes of the *Jesuit Relations* in Allan Greer, editor, *The Jesuit Relations: Natives and Missionaries in Seventeenth Century North America* (New York: Bedford/St. Martin's 2000) are aimed at college students. More information on Loyola and the Jesuits can be found on the Internet: www.jesuits.org.

Glossary

Alcalá, University of: a leading Spanish university, founded in 1508 and noted for its humanist curriculum. Loyola attended it 1526-1527.

Alumbrados: "The enlightened ones," Spanish religious dissidents hunted by the Inquisition. Some of the *Alumbrados* claimed such a close union with God that they did not need a church and could not sin.

Azpeitia: the Basque town near the French border where Loyola was born and raised.

Barcelona: the leading Spanish port on the Mediterranean. Loyola studied Latin there, 1524-1526.

Basques: a people with a unique language who have lived along the western border of France and Spain since prehistoric times. Loyola was a Basque.

Castle Loyola: the home of Loyola's family, located near Azpeitia.

Charles V (1500-58): the king of Spain (1516-56) and Holy Roman Emperor (1519-56), he also ruled Naples, Sicily, Milan, Austria, the Netherlands and much else in Europe and the Americas. Although a serious Catholic, he was lukewarm in supporting the Jesuits.

Courtiers: gentlemen who served as needed at the court of king and high officials.

Exercitants: people making the Spiritual Exercises.

Francis Xavier, Saint: Loyola's roommate at Paris. He was a pioneer Jesuit missionary in India, Indonesia, and Japan.

Guipúzcoa: Basque province of Spain where Loyola was born and raised.

Habsburg-Valois Wars: six wars (1521-26, 1527-29, 1536-38, 1542-44, 1546-47, and 1551-59) between the French Valois dynasty and the

Spanish-Austrian Habsburg dynast, fought largely over rival claims to territory in Italy. In several of these wars the French were allied with the Turks or the Lutheran Schmalkaldic League. These wars dominated Europe's political, diplomatic, and military history during Loyola's lifetime.

Holy Week: the week before Easter that includes many ceremonies commemorating the events leading up to the death of Jesus.

Inquisition: catholic agency used to repress heresy. The Spanish Inquisition, started in 1478, was under royal control. The Roman Inquisition, started in 1542, was under the pope. Inquisitors repeatedly examined and exonerated Loyola in both Spain and Italy.

Jesuits: the term "Jesuits" was first coined by their enemies. *See also* Society of Jesus.

Mass: the Roman Catholic celebration of the Lord's Supper or Eucharist.

Modus Parisiensis: a regular sequence of courses as taught at the University of Paris and later adapted in Jesuit schools.

Moors: Muslims in Spain and North Africa.

Pamplona: the capital of the Spanish province of Guipuzcoa where Loyola was wounded in 1521.

Paris, University of: Europe's leading university. Loyola studied there, 1528-1535.

Ratio Studiorum: the plan of studies employed in Jesuit schools. The final version was published in 1599 and was based in part on Loyola's Jesuit Constitutions.

Salamanca, University of: Spain's leading university, founded circa 1220, noted for scholastic philosophy and theology. Loyola studied there, 1527-28.

Schmalkaldic League: an alliance of German Lutheran cities and princes set up in 1531. The League fought two wars (1546-47 and 1552-55) against Charles V.

Society of Jesus: the official title of the Jesuit Order, founded at Rome by Loyola and his companions in 1540.

Spiritual Exercises: directions and rules with a planned set of meditations and mental prayers for guiding one's life to serve God. The Exercises were mapped out by Loyola and based on his own prayer experience. The full Exercises were to take roughly a month, but there were shorten versions.

The Spiritual Exercises: the manual written by Loyola and first printed in Latin at Rome in 1548. It was designed to help directors who were guiding exercitants through the Spiritual Exercises.

Index

194 ■ INDEX